new country garden

new country garden

ELSPETH THOMPSON   **MELANIE ECLARE**

RYLAND
PETERS
& SMALL

LONDON NEW YORK

Senior designer Sally Powell

Senior editor Clare Double

Location research manager Kate Brunt

Location researcher Jenny Drane

Production Patricia Harrington

Art director Gabriella Le Grazie

Publishing director Alison Starling

UK Locations Melanie Eclare and
Elspeth Thompson

Text by Elspeth Thompson

All photographs by Melanie Eclare

Front cover photograph: Sticky Wicket wildlife garden near Dorchester, designed and created by Peter and Pam Lewis. Back jacket: above left, Niall Manning and Alastair Morton's garden, Dunard, Fintry, Scotland; centre right, Jim Reynolds' garden 'Butterstream', Co. Meath, Ireland; below right, Sarah Raven's Cutting Garden in Brightling, designed by Sarah Raven.

First published in the United Kingdom in 2001

by Ryland Peters & Small
Kirkman House
12–14 Whitfield Street
London W1T 2RP
www.rylandpeters.com

10 9 8 7 6 5 4 3 2 1

For Frank and Tom

ISBN 1 84172 178 6

A CIP record for this book is available from the British Library.

Printed and bound in China

contents

introduction   6

PART ONE – THEMES   8

a plant lover's paradise   10

new formal gardens   30

family gardens   50

wildlife gardens   64

PART TWO – ELEMENTS   80

designing the garden   82

garden features   96

water features   114

perfect plants   122

directory   138

picture credits   140

index   142

acknowledgments   144

introduction

Until recently, the words 'new' and 'country' were not often heard together. For too long, we have tended to associate the country with all things traditional, and have looked for innovation in cities and towns. In gardening terms, 'country' has meant either old-fashioned cottage gardens, with familiar flowers and vegetables grown together in a colourful jumble, or a much grander style, where formal designs or naturalistic parkland linked large country houses with the landscape beyond.

Much has been made of today's renaissance in gardening: the flurry of new interest, in particular among young people, and the creation of stunning new gardens with a distinctive modern style. There is no doubt that garden design has caught up with architecture, interior design and fashion to become a truly contemporary form of expression. But most of the celebrated new gardens are town gardens – tiny spaces transformed into trendy outdoor dining rooms, or urban jungles crammed full of exotic plants and city salvage. You'd be forgiven for thinking that new ideas stopped short at the city limits. Meanwhile, however, another strand of garden design has been quietly taking root. Country dwellers have been just as inspired by recent developments in gardening, and have been creating wonderful gardens that are as exciting – and influential – as their urban counterparts. Call it new country, call it modern rustic, call it what you will – this new style of gardening has more to do with attitude and aesthetics than geographical location. And it is here to stay.

The new country garden hasn't turned its back on tradition entirely. You won't find here the plastic gardens, glass gardens, or metal and microchip gardens hailed as horticultural flavour of the month on television and in magazines. New materials undoubtedly have a place in the new country garden – concrete, slate and shiny new metal among them – but these are peaceful, laid-back places, where the important things in life such as beauty, comfort and romance are not forgotten.

The emphasis is on enjoyment: of the beautiful views beyond the boundary; of the changing atmospheres created by contrasting features and spaces; of the colours, shapes and textures of the plants themselves. Unlike many of the new urban gardens, these are gardeners' gardens. Their owners may not all be experts – although many of them are – but they are all united by a real love of plants and the magic they can weave. Yards of decking and limestone remain static and soulless without the textures, scents and shadows of well-chosen plants. And low-maintenance gardening is all very well – but where are the flowers?

Plants remain the real heart of the country-style garden. But you can forget about pastel sweet peas and pink cabbage roses. The palette and range of plants has been revolutionized, with bold clashing colours and a striking mix of heights and textures that breaks all the old rules. You'll find wildflower meadows, banks of ornamental grasses swaying in the breeze, even geometric beds filled with black and white irises – but what you won't find are plants that will struggle in the prevailing conditions. New country gardeners work with nature, not against it. And happy plants make a happy garden.

Design naturally plays a part in the new country garden – but never in an imposing, insensitive way that forgets the real purpose of the place. Gardens are to be looked at, certainly, but they are also to be lived in and enjoyed – not only by their creators and their families, friends and pets, but also by birds and other wildlife. The new country style fuses contemporary ideas with honest local materials to create spaces and features that relate to a relaxed and flexible modern way of life. It doesn't matter where you live – if you have ever longed for a pond buzzing with dragonflies, a swing in a tree overgrown with clematis and roses, or a modernday potager full of fresh organic vegetables, the new country garden is for you.

PART ONE

themes

a plant lover's paradise

new cottage-style gardens

bold plants in traditional beds

height, scale and colour run riot

new formal gardens

graphic topiary and evergreens

black and white

elegant modern parterres

family gardens

the sociable garden

space and swings for all

home-grown organic produce

wildlife gardens

swathes of grasses

self-seeding wildflower meadows

ponds buzzing with life

Left This cutting garden contains an exciting mix of large-scale plants, among them the silver Miss Willmott's ghost (*Eryngium giganteum*) and the huge purple spheres of *Allium giganteum* (foreground).
Below far left The splendid deep red blooms of the tall poppy *Papaver orientale* Goliath Group stand out against a green backdrop in this courtyard garden.
Below *Rosa* 'Lilli Marlene'.

a plant lover's paradise

Plants remain the heroes of the country-style garden: the heart and soul of the place and the real passion of its creators. But the palette of plants grown in these gardens has undergone a transformation. Colours are stronger and textures are bolder, while ornamental grasses bring a new sense of movement to beds and borders.

Below A modern colour mix in this impressive long border in Ireland, with its confident combination of bright shades and contrasting textures. The shaggy yellow daisies of *Inula hookeri* take up the rear, soaking up the sun behind mauve Michaelmas daisies, flaming orange crocosmias, delicate white spires of *Veronicastrum virginicum* and pink *Sidalcea malviflora*. The white flowers take on a luminous quality in the full sun, and the crocosmias' spear-like leaves are shot the brightest lime green.

Traditional cottage garden plants – sweet peas, hollyhocks, delphiniums and love-in-a-mist – are familiar to us all from old photographs and watercolours. Arranged with the tallest plants against the house wall and the rest in clouds of pastel pinks and blues in front, they create a picturesque patchwork that peaks in midsummer. The other timeless country garden image is the classic herbaceous border – strictly ordered in terms of height and subtle shifts of colour, and requiring a lot of maintenance. The new country garden takes the best from each of these traditional planting styles, but adds something of its own. Planting is bigger and bolder and breaks many of the old rules.

First, though, one of the most important lessons to re-learn from the old cottage gardeners is only to grow plants that will thrive in your conditions. The new country gardener is not interested in trying to grow rhododendrons or heather on chalky soil – in fact, he or she is probably not interested in growing rhododendrons or heather at all. Gardeners are resourceful souls – and over

Right Bold planting in terms of height, shape and colour prevails in this garden in East Sussex, specially created to provide flowers for cutting and arranging. Towering onopordums and cardoons are silhouetted against the sky, their scrolling silvery foliage providing a foil for the brilliant colours of the flowers – bright orange lilies, lime-green euphorbias and violet alliums.
Below The exotic, speckled orange flowers of turk's-head lilies create a fiery combination with the scarlet *Crocosmia* 'Lucifer'.

Right Soft plumes of the Mexican feather grass *Stipa tenuissima* catch the light beautifully amid clouds of pale pink astrantia. The delicate starry flowers and wispy grass perfectly complement each other in this stunning wild garden in Dorset.
Left Bright red *Persicaria amplexicaulis*, fuzzy mauve Joe Pye weed (*Eupatorium purpureum*) and purple monardas form bold swathes towards the back of this border, a splendid contrast with the lime-green euphorbia in the foreground.
Below In this beautiful Irish country garden, a few strong plants grow in bold masses to great effect, among them a white yarrow (*Achillea ptarmica* 'The Pearl'), purple loosestrife (*Lythrum salicaria*), pink phlox, delphiniums and eryngiums.

the years have found ways to create artificial conditions in even the most unpromising soils and sites, but in recent years there has been a welcome return to the principles of suiting your planting to your surroundings. Natural-looking plants that at least give the impression they might be indigenous to the area now hold sway. Inspired by examples such as Beth Chatto's gravel and damp gardens in East Anglia and the designer Isabelle Greene's work in arid California, gardeners are realizing that there is no substitute for a plant that is truly happy in its natural habitat. Growth will be stronger, flowers larger and more plentiful – and there may also be advantages in terms of design, as plants which associate naturally together are often their best aesthetic partners, too.

Above The tiny blue annual sweet pea, *Lathyrus sativus*, is an unusual choice for these plant supports.

Below The wonderful dusky pink oriental poppy 'Patty's Plum' is one of the many intense, slightly sombre shades used to good effect in this garden in Holland, along with indigo monkshood (*Aconitum*) and the deep crimson astrantia, *Astrantia major* 'Hadspen Blood'.

So let soil and conditions be your starting point. The style of the garden and its planting will be dictated by what you find. Soil-testing kits which indicate whether your soil is acid or alkaline are available from garden centres, and come with clear instructions, but you will find out just as much, if not more, by looking hard at the soil and its structure, and by studying the surrounding gardens and talking to their owners. Often a garden will have more than one natural habitat, so think about how to incorporate these into the overall design. A sunbaked south-facing terrace near the house would be a perfect spot for Mediterranean-style plantings of silver-leaved plants and aromatic herbs, for instance; and where the soil is very poor, you could create a gravel garden with plants that will thrive in the shallowest, driest soils. There may be dry shade under large trees, or a more fertile, but nonetheless shady, woodland area just waiting for spring bulbs, bluebells and ferns. A high water table or a stream in the garden will bring its own opportunities and challenges.

Don't feel that this approach to planting is limiting to your garden's potential. Within the constraints of what is naturally feasible, you are absolutely free to create the garden of your dreams – and remember that happy plants make a happy garden.

Right In one half of this Wiltshire courtyard garden, geometric beds have been devoted to white and natural-coloured plants. Here, white 'Iceberg' roses mingle with the sweet-scented white rocket *Hesperis matronalis* var. *albiflora*, while the giant feather grass *Stipa gigantea* makes a golden spray on the left – the same warm colour as the sunlit stone walls. The whole composition in shades of white, green and gold is simple yet subtly satisfying – a perfect blend of plants and existing architecture.
Left Rambling and climbing roses festoon a series of arches in another Dutch garden, underplanted with frothy London pride (*Saxifraga* x *urbium*).

Left *Crambe cordifolia* is a stunning plant for the new country garden, creating clouds of starry white flowers filling an area of 1.8 m (6 ft) high and wide. Here it mingles well with frothy white mock orange (*Philadelphus*).

Right In the same garden, a wonderful mix of white valerian (*Centranthus ruber* 'Albus') and clary sage (*Salvia sclarea* var. *turkestanica*) is crowned by a backlit fountain of *Stipa gigantea*. This trio is particularly well matched in terms of form, colour and texture. *Salvia sclarea* var. *turkestanica* is excellent for new perennial-style gardens. Its pale bracts and pink-flecked flowers on tall stems have an architectural quality, and look good at every stage in their development, from sculptural pendent buds to the dried autumn flower heads. A traditional cottage garden plant, it can also look surprisingly modern. The velvety heart-shaped leaves are also attractive.

Colour in the new country garden can be bolder than in traditional schemes. Don't be scared to use combinations that were once deemed clashing: reds next to bright pinks and oranges, for instance, or purples with magenta and lime green. Christopher Lloyd at Great Dixter in East Sussex caused a stir when he replaced his rose garden with scarlet canna lilies (*Canna* x *generalis*) and flame-coloured dahlias some years ago, but these bright, even brash colours are now firmly in fashion. You may even want to devote a special late summer 'Hot Border' to such plants, with red hot pokers, tawny heleniums and rudbeckias, orange and red daylilies, dahlias like the scarlet 'Bishop of Llandaff' with its contrasting dark stems and leaves, and sprays of *Crocosmia* 'Lucifer' like fireworks in the foreground. Intersperse your hot-coloured planting with cooler-coloured grasses and foliage plants if you need to tone things down.

There has been a huge interest in dark-coloured plants in recent years – in purples so deep they are almost black (as in the gorgeous, much-sought-after iris, 'Black Knight') or the intense velvety reds of *Knautia macedonica*, the daylily *Hemerocallis* 'Little Grapette' or the lovely *Astrantia major* 'Hadspen Blood'. These can create sumptuous effects in the garden not unlike those in Venetian paintings – and contrary to what one might expect, their colours glow richly from the gloomiest shadows. Black and white or silver plants are also popular in new country gardens, and can be used with great wit and style – alternating squares of the strappy black grass *Ophiopogon planiscapus* 'Nigrescens' with the soft silvery lamb's-ear leaves of *Stachys byzantina*, to form a chessboard effect, for instance, or pots of the near-black tulip 'Queen of Night' interspersed with others of *Tulipa* 'Spring Green', its milky petals shot with fresh green. Some

Left The wonderful rambling rose, 'Paul's Himalayan Musk', swamps a potting shed with fragrant soft pink flowers in this Dutch country garden. Though it flowers for just a few weeks of the year, the effect is extraordinarily beautiful, making it a firm favourite among climbing roses. It can also be trained up trees or to form fragrant floral swags between branches or buildings.

More evidence that pastels can create splendid modern effects.

Far left Giant scabious, *Cephalaria gigantea*, is a robust and handsome plant, forming a large open clump in this Dorset plantswoman's garden. Its pale lemon flowers are borne on stems up to 2.4 m (8 ft) high, but its semi-transparent habit, waving and trembling in the slightest breeze, means that it can look equally at home at the front or back of the border. It needs room to spread: each plant forms a clump 1.2 m (4 ft) wide, with dark green deep-cut leaves.

Left In the same garden, pale blue delphinium hybrids look beautiful but ghostly in the low light.

plants have this coveted black and white colouring within the same flower – think of black and white pansies, or the chequerboard *Aquilegia* 'Magpie'.

White-flowering plants will never go out of style – but instead of traditional 'White Gardens', such as the one made famous by Vita Sackville-West at Sissinghurst and much copied ever since, today's country gardeners are creating 'Moon Gardens' filled with pale flowers and foliage that will be seen at their best beneath a summer full moon. Silver and grey foliage plants such as lavenders, *Santolina*, beautiful *Convolvulus cneorum* with its pink-tinged, bell-like flowers and certain sages, including Russian sage (*Perovskia* 'Blue Spire'), have an integral place in Mediterranean-style and seaside gardens, but are also good foils for some of the deeper pinks and purples. The other great new foliage colour is chartreuse – that seductive greeny-yellow ranging from the sharp lime greens of *Alchemilla mollis* and the

golden hop, *Humulus lupulus* 'Aureus', to the duller olive-grey foliage of *Helleborus foetidus* and some euphorbias. It can provide interesting contrasts, both with other greens and hot reds, pinks and oranges.

These hot new colour combinations work so well partly because planting patterns themselves have become bolder. The old-style herbaceous borders relied on small groupings of different plants, perhaps repeated at intervals, while too many sudden contrasts were frowned on. Nowadays, the trend is for bold sweeps and swathes of colour, so that one type of plant runs into the next, and the combinations are constantly shifting as you walk past. Instead of the strict traditional division between lawn, paths and borders, go for an effect more akin to that of an abstract painting. A wonderful effect can be achieved with just a handful of different plants, used over quite a large area, but giving interesting contrasts in texture, leaf shape and height. The natural clump- or tussock-forming habits of hardy

Above *Sidalcea malviflora* combines an unusual mixture of strong structure with soft delicate colour – a useful modern border plant with flowers that last.

Right A pretty mixture of pink foxgloves, lavender and white bleeding heart (*Dicentra spectabilis* 'Alba') thrives in a corner of this former farmyard in Wiltshire, in the shade of a huge copper beech (*Fagus sylvatica* f. *purpurea*). The foxgloves have self-seeded towards the front of the beds, living proof that tall plants need not be confined to the back of the border. The old stone walls, covered in moss and lichen, provide the perfect backdrop for plants.

geraniums, for instance, or fountain grasses can be exploited, with drifts of taller, wispier plants infiltrating their ranks. No need to keep tall specimens to the back: spires of foxgloves, delphiniums, monkshood, foxtail lilies or the towering silvery thistle-like Miss Willmott's ghost (*Eryngium giganteum*) work like vertical punctuation marks among the mounds of lower-growing plants. Climbing plants such as roses and clematis can also add height if they are grown up simple obelisks or painted metal supports. The effects work just as well in a formal-style garden, contained within simple geometric beds.

The aim is to build up a shimmering, shifting canvas of plants in which one species is viewed against, or through another. Spindly plants with a 'see-through' habit are useful here – *Verbena bonariensis*, with its tiny purple flower heads on branching architectural stems; fuzzy *Thalictrum delavayi*; or the giant scabious, *Cephalaria gigantea*, with papery, pale lemon flowers, can even be used in the foreground, where they will create an organza-like effect, sending wild, wayward stems in every direction. Where the old-style border would have a wall at the back and a viewing path along the front, this new looser style can work without a backdrop, and with narrow gravel paths leading right in and through the planting if required. Planting *en masse* has other advantages. If you like lots of flowers in the house, you will always have enough to pick, with no fear of depleting your display. There has been a recent return to the idea of a cutting garden, where all your favourite flowers are grown in a colourful patchwork – not unlike a vegetable plot – with the sole aim of picking to arrange inside. But if you do not have room for a separate cutting area, bold masses of annuals and perennials spread in swathes throughout the garden should ensure a plentiful supply.

One of the most exciting developments in gardening in recent years is the increasing popularity of what has become known as the 'new perennial' style, which makes bold use of ornamental grasses. Building on the principle of using the right

plants for the right place, this style of gardening was first espoused by the German gardener and ecologist Karl Foerster at the turn of the last century and is now common in German parks and gardens, and gaining ground in Holland (where Piet Oudolf has his well-known nursery). In the United States, James van Sweden and the German-born Wolfgang Oehme are converting lawn-loving Americans back to prairie-style plants.

With its emphasis on sculptural grasses and wild-looking clumps of perennials, new perennial planting has a naturalistic beauty which is particularly suited to new country gardens. Grasses grow well in most soils and conditions, and their strappy frond-like leaves and feathery flower heads introduce an exciting range of textures, which are particularly valuable in late summer when many other plants are fading. Of all garden plants, these are the most responsive to changes in light, so place them where the low afternoon sun can shine right through them. A shaft of sunlight illuminating a large clump of *Stipa gigantea* has an effect akin to fireworks, while the pale plumes of pennisetums form a fuzzy golden halo. As the sun moves around and through the different grasses, it will highlight their different shapes and textures. Some, like *Calamagrostis* x *acutiflora* 'Stricta' have a firm upright habit; others, such as the deschampsias, create graceful arcs above the surrounding foliage, like living fountains. The summer-flowering feather grass, *Stipa tenuissima*, has fluffy fronds like tousled fine hair, while *Pennisetum orientale* has fuzzy, furry foxtail seed-heads, and the clump-forming carexes have twirling, twisting tendrils. Their beauty is only intensified by a white outline of winter frost.

Grasses also bring a ravishing sense of movement to the garden, as their swaying foliage and feather-light plumes respond to the slightest breeze. Though most often combined with herbaceous perennials and other wild-looking plants, they are increasingly used to great effect within the clipped hedges and geometric beds of formal gardens, where they soften the boundaries and animate an otherwise static scene.

Left A stunning mixture of alliums and grasses in this modern Wiltshire garden. The pale arching fronds of pheasant's tail grass (*Stipa arundinacea*) in the foreground contrast with the strappy bronze leaves of the New Zealand flax (*Phormium tenax* 'Purpureum') and the silvery wisps of *Stipa tenuissima* to the right. *Stipa gigantea* towers above them all, its oat-like seed-heads lit by the sun and waving in the breeze. This combination of grasses sits well against a backdrop of fields.
Below Dark maroon flowers of *Geranium phaeum* in the foreground; arching sprays of *Buddleia alternifolia* make a fountain effect in the distance.

A consummate piece of planting in this Dorset garden. The wild natural effect belies the skill in orchestrating these concentric circles. In the centre is a chamomile lawn, and around that a ring of self-seeded cloud grass mixed with low-growing purple-flowering thymes. A further circle of grasses and low-growing silver-leaved plants is punctuated by spheres of *Allium cristophii*, adding a vertical element to the composition, while spires of foxgloves rise up from mounds of cranesbill geraniums and oregano in the foreground. Gravel paths run between the beds like those in a low foot maze.

Above Arches tumbling with climbing and rambling roses lead the way to the lawn in this romantic Dutch garden.

Top right Blue agapanthus and white rose bay willowherb (*Epilobium angustifolium*) are among the strong plants fighting for space in this spectacular Irish border. Wine-red buttons of *Knautia macedonica* weave among the purple loosestrife (*Lythrum salicaria*) and white campanulas (*C. lactiflora*).

Right Drifts of pink scabious, purple lupins, and the mauve geranium 'Johnson's Blue' look gloriously wild in this Dutch garden, with pink *Rosa rugosa* forming a backdrop. Pale lemon *Cephalaria gigantea* towers at the back, while among the sea of flowers and foliage ornamental alliums such as *A. cristophii* are emerging. Like everything in this garden, the effect looks wonderfully spontaneous, but is in fact carefully maintained.

Grasses remind us of the rhythms of plants in the wild landscape beyond the garden borders – of the wind rippling through fields of oats or rye, or rustling the tufts of thrift on sand dunes. The swishing of their leaves can also bring the ocean to mind.

Grasses grow easily in almost all soil types and require next to no maintenance. But combining them with other plants to create a year-round effect can be hard to get right. They are often grown in a separate area of the garden geared to peak in late summer and autumn. To extend the interest for as many months of the year as possible, think of grasses emerging from layers of contrasting flowers and foliage. Tall, swaying *Miscanthus sinensis* could shoot up from swathes of the daisy-like flowers of rudbeckia, for instance, providing foliage contrast in spring and a splash of bright yellow flowers in summer, while in autumn, the dried dark cones of the rudbeckia flowers will be silhouetted against the pale, silky ribbons of the grass seed-heads, just waiting for an outline of frost. Or how about the graceful arching stems of *Stipa calamagrostis* swaying above white-starred domes of *Anaphalis triplinervis* (pearly everlasting) and clouds of vivid mauve asters?

Plants that extend the season with dried leaves, attractive flower heads and seeds are crucial to this style of gardening. Piet Oudolf once said, only half jokingly, that a plant is not worth growing unless it looks good when it is dead – and the beauty of dying flowers, frosted leaves and gaunt stems is part of the new perennial aesthetic. *Echinacea*, *Anaphalis*, *Sedum* and *Origanum* produce long-lasting flower heads which look good all winter long – as well as being appreciated by the birds – and most of the grasses will hold their heads right through the winter. So resist the temptation to wield the shears until February, and then it will be only a few weeks before the new spring foliage starts to appear. For a totally year-round garden,

you can fill that gap by underplanting with a carpet of spring bulbs, and perhaps some drumstick alliums for early summer, when the grasses are about knee high. But once they take off you can just stand back and enjoy the show.

The looser, more relaxed style of planting outlined in this chapter has the advantage of being low maintenance. As you are fighting neither the natural conditions in your garden nor the natural growth habits and requirements of the plants, your new country garden should be much easier to maintain than the traditional herbaceous border, while its flowering season is much longer than that of the old-style cottage garden. Leaving plants to seed is not only a boon to the wildlife in your garden, it may also result in some surprises the following year, as old favourites crop up in unexpected places.

Formal designs bring a timeless sense of beauty and order to the garden. Move the formal garden firmly into the twenty-first century by pairing clipped hedges and geometric beds with wild naturalistic planting and ornamental grasses that spill over the edges and sway in the breeze.

new formal gardens

Left Topiary gardens are not always strictly clipped and tidied. In this garden, the woolly new growth on beech and box hedging creates a softer, more romantic atmosphere. **Right** In this courtyard garden enclosed by stone farm buildings, simple square beds edged in box are 'containers' for colourful, exuberant planting which spills over onto the grass paths in high summer. White and pale colours are confined to one side of the garden, while this side is devoted to hot reds and rich deep shades – the clipped box provides the perfect foil for the clouds of flowers and sprays of ornamental grasses. The central mulberry tree rises from a plinth-like square of clipped box.

A more formal style of gardening, with a strong geometric structure laid out in paths and beds, often outlined in low evergreen hedging, suits all types of architecture, from medieval cottages to Georgian townhouses and much later styles. A new formal garden is also the perfect complement to the clean lines of contemporary architecture. These formal gardens need not be the enclosed, even forbidding places that were once cultivated between high hedges or walls. There is something timeless and calming about a garden laid out in clipped box and yew – and it looks good all year round, especially after a hoar frost or light fall of snow.

Ordered formality has played a part in garden design from its earliest origins in the terraced water gardens of Persia and Mogul India. From the tiny enclosed herb or physic gardens of medieval monasteries to the radiating pathways of Versailles, earlier formal gardens were usually an attempt to create an earthly expression of a heavenly or metaphysical order – whether found in the healing powers of plants or the divine right of kings. Classical rules of scale, proportion and symmetry were brought into play with this end in view. The results were almost always designed to be seen from above – either by God or from an upstairs window – and there is no doubt that they were impressive, if at times a little rigid.

Contemporary gardening still has a place for formality. Indeed, a strong formal layout, coupled with the restrained use of a few well-chosen plants, makes the perfect setting for today's pared-down sense of style. But, as is the case with planting styles, some important changes have taken place. In particular, interesting new materials and a dynamic sense of movement have revolutionized the formal garden and brought it firmly into the twenty-first century. Now it is by no means unheard of to have formal gardens featuring concrete or

Left and above A strictly symmetrical layout of curved beds around a central water feature might traditionally have been planted with low-growing herbaceous plants in pastel colours. In this exciting Herefordshire garden it gives the structural setting for an exuberant mixture of ornamental grasses and wild-looking perennials – a striking modern contrast that is very much in keeping with the spirit of the new country style. Height is provided by the towering

seed-heads of *Stipa gigantea* and by metal obelisks, symmetrically placed to anchor the design. As one wanders around the paths between the beds, the colours and textures of the plants can be appreciated in ever-shifting combinations. The geometric elements of this garden are maintained meticulously, which provides a satisfying contrast with the clouds of billowing plants – grass paths are closely mown, making a clear axis to lead the eye down to the little folly at the far end, while the hedges that contain this densely planted area will be clipped straight once they reach the required height. Small formal gardens such as this look stunning viewed from an upstairs window.

Right Box (*Buxus*) is one of the most commonly used plants for topiary – its evergreen leaves and dense habit make it ideal. For a contemporary look, forget complex fiddly designs and stick to simple graphic shapes such as spheres and cubes. Clipped plants in containers are useful for flanking paths or entrances and creating instant order against a backdrop of wilder, more naturalistic planting. They can be moved around the garden to create different effects throughout the year, and can go with you when you move house.

even glass. Modern materials such as galvanized
metal or plastic may be used as containers or as
edgings for formal beds, while spaces in between may
be filled with slate chippings or pebbles. In a 'modern
rustic' take on the parterre, beds can even be edged
in woven hazel or willow. Where traditional formal
gardens were flat and static, today's versions are
often strongly sculptural, at times incorporating
contemporary art works into the design; at others
repeating simple geometric shapes – clipped box
cubes or lollipops of bay or privet, for instance –
rhythmically across a given area. There is often
a vertical element to the design – smart wooden
obelisks with white roses trained up them, say,
or a long arched pergola covered with a grapevine.

One of the most interesting and influential
developments in the new country garden has been
the fusion of a formal layout with the wilder, exuberant
style of planting described in the previous chapter.
Soft mounds or fuzzy clouds of flowers and foliage
spill over hedges or edges and blur the boundaries in
a beguiling haze of colour, while swaying, shimmering
grasses provide the perfect foil to all those straight
lines and trimmed shapes.

Formality in the new country garden is not just
to be looked at. There is no place here for sterile
arrangements of clipped plants and potted shrubs,
looking like the pieces in a permanently interrupted
game of chess. In today's more relaxed style of
gardening, formal design principles and features are
harnessed to create useful spaces and atmospheric
effects. In a smaller walled garden or terrace near
the house, a formal design can create a real 'outside
room' for living and eating outdoors, with floor, walls

and even a 'ceiling' in the form of a pergola or vine-clad wires overhead. In larger areas the illusion of a living maze of plants and sculpted elements builds up intrigue and mystery. While the layout of traditional gardens meant that visitors to the garden often knew exactly where a path would lead, new formal gardens are places for exploration. Even from inside the house, an avenue of junipers, clipped to form the pillars of a living colonnade, may coax you out to discover a secret seat at the far end. Or a rose-clad pergola intersecting two areas of the garden may tempt you to turn off to one side, to discover a new feature or admire a hidden view.

　　Old-style formal gardens were often rather intricate affairs. Larger gardens were criss-crossed with complicated paths and secondary axes; smaller parterres had their compartments filled with a froth of different flowering plants or coloured gravels. The key to the contemporary formal garden is simplicity. Stunningly effective gardens can be created using only two or three types of plant, the interest lying in the contrasting shapes and different shades of green, and in shadows cast at different times of day.

Above In this formal rose garden in Herefordshire, evergreen topiary shapes are being trained within simple home-made wooden obelisks – attractive features in themselves which echo the pointed gables of the summerhouse beyond. Symmetrically placed, they animate the garden, almost like sculpture, all year, providing interest after the roses have faded.

Left Chunky evergreen hedges can be used to create a sense of intimacy and enclosure in a garden; they also shelter tender plants from harsh winds.

Right This stunning formal rose garden in Scotland has a simple layout of four rectangular beds around a central sundial. Low clipped box hedges surround the beds like picture frames. Among a foaming sea of low-growing perennials, metal obelisks painted a contrasting dark blue rise up like the masts of ships, planted with climbing roses and clematis. These low clipped hedges form an enclosing windbreak; any higher and they would shut out the view, which forms a stunning backdrop to the garden.

Left Simple graphic designs are the trademark of new formal style. In this Dutch garden a composition of clipped box in straight lines, swirls and low mounds creates a marvellous feeling of calm. Frequent pruning is needed to preserve the look.

Below and right When choosing plants for modern formal gardens, look for those with a strong graphic structure. The delicate hooked petals of the chequered *Aquilegia* 'Magpie' (below) are a work of art in themselves, as are the deep purple interlocking sections of a Roman artichoke (right). These sultry dark colours are not only fashionable, but they stand out surprisingly well against a backdrop of evergreen hedges, which can frame the flowers like pictures. Intersperse with ornamental grasses for a wilder, naturalistic combination.

Simple allées of hawthorn hedges or pleached limes need lead nowhere in particular to invite exploration; the simple enjoyment of sunlight dappled through green leaves overhead and dewy wet grass underfoot can be all the more intense without added distractions. Standard bay trees growing amid squares or circles of clipped box can look wonderfully sculptural against a background of slate or gravel chippings: in spring, the fresh bright green growth on the box will add a whole new dimension to the garden. And for a modern interpretation of the parterre, plant formal edged beds with a sweep of one type or colour of flower – black or white tulips in late spring, for instance, or long-flowering annuals such as *Cosmos* all summer. Or, for the most dramatic contrast of shape and texture, opt for swathes of shimmering ornamental grasses. This approach can work especially well near to the house, linking the formal garden with the wilder landscape beyond the domestic boundaries.

Think, too, of the parts of the formal garden that are not filled in with plants. York stone, limestone, slate and gravel are good foils for formal designs, but there are many other possibilities. Bricks and tiles can be

laid in attractive patterns to complement the planting. Or how about a pebble mosaic, with stones of different colours set in swirls or stripes in cement? Chequerboard designs with alternate squares filled with low-growing plants and 'hard' landscaping materials are always eye-catching – try short grasses, sempervivums (houseleeks), chamomile or thyme interspersed with white pebbles, seashells or silvery driftwood. The alternatives are endless.

When planning a formal garden, it is essential to sit down with a pencil and paper and sketch out an overall design, rather than just plunging in and creating a bed here

Left This formal garden in Herefordshire is as rich and exquisite as a jewel-box. The effect is crowded, but never chaotic, as a framework of clipped box hedges and mounds keeps a picturesque mix of apricot roses, fennel and catmint (*Nepeta*) under control. Columns of fastigiate yew mark the entrances and corners, while pots of regale lilies surround the central pond. Seen from an upstairs window, the garden is spread out on the lawn like a piece of decorative embroidery, the perfect contrast to the countryside beyond the fence.

and a water feature there. Begin from the house, considering the views from the doorways and most important rooms. Think about the main axes of the garden, the principal paths, beds and other components. Taking some of their measurements from the house will help anchor the house more subtly in its surroundings: the width of walls or windows, for instance, could be echoed in features on the ground. There may be elements in the nearby landscape you wish to bring into the garden by means of 'orchestrated views' – a church spire on a hilltop, or a circle of trees on a distant ridge. You can then create vistas to focus the eye, by planting hedges or laying paths in these directions, and pruning trees and foliage to open up the views. Some of the traditional characteristics of the formal garden, such as terraces, hedges, allées and rills, can be used to provide links between different levels or separate areas (for more ideas see *Designing the Garden*, page 82).

Where the traditional formal garden was always strictly symmetrical, modern interpretations need not be so constrained. The layout can be much more abstract – either on graphic lines, like a Mondrian painting, with an underlying tension present between its irregularly shaped elements, or taking inspiration from the organic flowing spaces of Zen gardens. Formal gardens usually mean straight lines and right angles, but there is space in the new country style for sweeping curves, circles, zigzags and crescent moons. Spiral designs recur in gardens of all periods and cultures and can be particularly powerful. Some of these

Left The new formal garden isn't just about straight lines and right angles – find room for curves, circles and spirals too. In this modern Wiltshire garden, a perfect circle of lawn is outlined in box hedging, creating curved beds for pretty cottage-style planting behind. On the right, the curve is taken up in dry stone walling, with beds built into the top for rock plants. The circle sweeps round to a gravel garden in the foreground full of sun lovers such as the orange poppy *Papaver spicatum*, *Origanum* 'Kent Beauty' and eschscholzias. The strong shapes and colours of foxtail lilies (*Eremurus*) and a bronze phormium stand out against the backdrop of the lawn and bring some structure to the surrounding planting.

Above A symphony of soft mauves and rich pinks sits well against the textured greens and clipped box hedges in this courtyard garden in Wiltshire. Note the pleasing variety of shapes – the column of clipped juniper, the squat chunks of hedging, the spears of crocosmia leaves and the openwork metal column up which a dark red rose is climbing – and the contrasting textures of the foliage. Among these, the spires of purple lupins repeat the shape of the juniper behind – visual echoes such as this create subtle aesthetic undercurrents around the garden, like recurring phrases in music.

Left Although often thought of as cottage-style plants, lupins have a strong architectural structure and can look surprisingly modern in the right environment. Choose the deeper reds, mauves, and plain white and creams instead of pale pinks and lemons.

Left and above Training plants into standards (ball shapes on top of a long straight stem) can be an attractive way to bring structure to a garden. Plants to train include roses, as in this intimate courtyard garden (left), while bay (*Laurus nobilis*, above) lends itself well to the standard shape, and looks good either in a formal border or a kitchen garden.

shapes will make simple 'foot mazes' – patterns on the ground composed of low-growing plants and grasses.

Do not feel you should fill every space with plants. Empty areas play an important part in the new formal garden, and have a strong aesthetic and emotional impact. They create the 'breathing spaces' in a walk around the garden – the horticultural equivalent of a sorbet to clear the palate between the courses of a meal. There can be few things more beautiful than a square pool in a simple hedged space, with just a single jet of water springing up into the sky. Encountered after a much more colourful and crowded area of the garden, such a space is like a lungful of fresh air.

As formal gardens do not rely on flowers for their beauty, they look good all year round. The layout of paths and structural plants will generate an atmosphere in all lights and seasons – magical in frost or snow, freshly greened in spring or shadowy and mysterious after dark. Evergreens are most commonly used for hedges and topiary, but even more seasonal contrasts can be had by using deciduous plants. Beech and hawthorn, for instance, are striking at all stages of their development. When summer is over, the coppery autumn leaves hang on until well into the winter, when the bare branches create a stark beauty all their own, and the new leaves in spring are like tatters of lime silk. Deciduous hedges can be used to create areas of the garden that are 'transparent' in winter – an outside room containing a sculpture or oversized urn, for instance, which is concealed by foliage at other times. A tree or shrub with bright winter berries or foliage would make a good centrepiece for such a garden within the garden.

Formal gardens are often associated with scented plants – herb wheels or rose gardens in particular. As well as providing a pleasing contrast between the different types of foliage and flowers, edged beds may help contain the fragrance of these plants, and will also keep spreaders like mint and *Nepeta* under control. Formal beds are also good foils for plants such as

Below A combination of formal box hedges and stylish containers has been laid out in part of this Irish garden rather like furniture in an outdoor room. Terracotta planters are raised on blocks to be visible above the neatly clipped box, and flank the gravel path at regular intervals. The pots are planted with white daisies, but could be replanted to give a seasonal display throughout the year, with crocus or narcissus to flower in spring – just one type of flower for all the pots works best. Indeed, restraining the colour scheme to green and white throughout creates an atmosphere of peace and harmony. The painted metal bench at the end of the path must be a lovely place to sit with a book or a drink.

Right Modern architecture in this Californian garden meant the opportunity to be especially bold with its design. In a hot climate, white concrete walls are the perfect backdrop for climbing vines or just the wonderful shadows of the plants. The trunks of a row of almond trees have been painted white, to match the retaining walls (and protect against pests). The hard landscaping in this garden is all straight lines and sharp angles, which makes the wild, wayward shapes of the plants stand out all the more.

poppies and old roses whose appeal is strictly seasonal. When such blooms are at their ephemeral best, the fragile flowers billow like pale luminous clouds above the dark evergreen hedges, softening their edges and blurring the boundaries. After the flowers have faded, the beds' geometric shapes still remain.

The words 'rustic' and 'formal' may not often crop up in the same sentence, but some of the principles of formal gardening may be useful to you even if your taste is much more relaxed and traditionally country in style. Classical proportion and symmetry have survived the centuries just *because* they are so satisfying and easy on the eye; they can be even more enchanting in unexpected surroundings. Classical placings and pairings will always have an impact – but

Above Clipped box hedges contain a rich variety of plant shapes, colours and textures, including the orange-flowered euphorbia, *E. griffithii*, red *Lychnis chalcedonica* and deep red roses. The pale stone of the surrounding buildings creates a light backdrop for these deep, rich colours.

Right The sombre dark reds, purples, bronzes and near-blacks in this stunning Herefordshire border complement the Gothic arches of the pavilion beyond, as do the minaret heads on the topiary hedges.

try to give them a quirky modern twist. Where a traditional design might have a Gothic seat set in a niche in a high clipped yew hedge, why not install a simple bleached wood throne in its own twiggy arbour, flanked by a pair of large potted shrubs? A retro stone urn at the end of a vista could be replaced by a modern version in slate, or a simple cairn of stones. And whether you are planting trees or placing tubs on a terrace, pairs or groups of four make a conventionally formal effect, while threes, fives and sevens may be more dynamic.

Being creative with the mower can create interesting effects: imagine a circular glade in the woods, surrounded by ferns and wild flowers – a magical spot for a picnic. In an orchard, leave squares of longer grass around the trees in spring, and plant snowdrops and *Iris sibirica*. Or try making a 'sacred grove' using a simple circle of woodland trees such as silver birch. In his wonderful sculpture garden, Little Sparta in Scotland, the artist Ian Hamilton Finlay has accessorized his grove with a stone inscription saying 'Bring Back the Birch'.

Humour and trickery were traditionally part of the formal garden – remember the *giochi d'acqua* or water games of Italian Renaissance gardens that would soak the unsuspecting visitor who trod on certain stones? There is plenty of scope for wit and whimsy in the modern formal garden. Rather than jets of water, why not use modern technology and have steam vapour set on a timer to turn on unexpectedly? Or create exciting lighting effects after dark, projecting coloured images onto walls or lawns. Play games

Right Training roses up a painted metal obelisk gives height to this formal bed, as do the pink and white foxgloves that have self-seeded in front. Foxgloves (*Digitalis*) are useful plants in the new formal garden. Though originally woodland plants, their spires of bell-like flowers bring an air of unpredictable elegance to the garden in late spring and summer.

Far right White-spotted foxgloves such as *Digitalis purpurea* 'Pam's Choice' are particularly beautiful – this one grows up to 3 m (10 ft) tall.

Above More foxgloves in the foreground of this modern Wiltshire garden. This view illustrates the garden's masterful design, with a patchwork of square beds and grassy paths in what was once a farmyard. Plants traditionally associated with formal gardens, such as clipped box, junipers and lavender are combined with cottage-garden flowers like nepeta and huge towering grasses. The enormous bronze *Phormium tenax* in the background is a bold move, its spiky silhouette sitting well against the sunbaked stone walls. Lavender is another useful plant in formal gardens. Trimmed after flowering, it can be used to create hedges and strong boxy effects, while left to its own devices, the flower heads make a lovely purple haze above the glaucous grey-green leaves. There are hundreds of lavenders, in every shade from white through pinks and mauves to deep indigo-purple. Pruning will stop them growing leggy and woody in the centre, but never cut back to bare wood or growth will not sprout back.

Right Steps lead up to an open studio door in this Californian garden. Wisps of *Stipa tenuissima* waft over the edges on the left – this is a good grass for softening the harsh lines of hard landscaping. On the right, the leaves of a Japanese acer are shot with sunshine, while asparagus ferns and irises thrive in the warm climate.

Above Throughout the history of garden design, plants have been used to create structured vistas and frame selected views. In this modern formal design in Ireland, well-grown specimens of Irish yew (*Taxus baccata* 'Fastigiata') create a classical colonnade, leading the eye to a decorative water feature at the end of the path.

Right In this romantic Dutch parterre garden, roses trained over a metal arch form an exquisite surround for a view of a pretty stone fountain, making one pause to drink in its beauty before going up the steps.

with scale, placing enormous oversized urns in a tiny area, for instance, or using false perspectives. Tapered paths and narrowing pools can make a short garden seem longer, while the ingenious use of mirrors can extend it indefinitely. Framed by arches or door frames in a wall – even an old window frame salvaged from a skip – mirrors really do create the illusion of a new space beyond. They also give you more garden for your money. Run a rill edged with formal hedging right up flush to a mirror in a wall and you double its length; place two mirrors set at right angles in front of a few small clipped yews and you have a full-scale formal garden for the price of a few plants. Mirrors work best set at an angle away from the viewer. Any illusion will be broken if you see yourself reflected too soon in the proceedings; you need to keep a few tricks up your sleeve.

family gardens

The new country garden is a sociable place, filled
with children, pets and streams of weekend visitors.
A well-designed space can double effortlessly as
an outdoor sitting room and dining room as well
as a children's living playground – and don't forget
to make room for an organic kitchen garden.

The key to designing a garden for all the family is
flexibility. Rather than creating fixed and permanent
areas for eating out, playing games or watching the
sunset, try to build change and adaptability into
the design. All functional areas – barbecues,
climbing frames and vegetable plots alike –
should be attractive features in their own right, and
contribute to the overall look and feel of the garden.

Top A shingled summerhouse makes a great play house or spot for adults to enjoy a drink.
Above In a hot arid climate, some sort of shade within the garden is not only welcome
but essential. This corner beneath the fig tree in California would be a lovely place for an
alfresco lunch at the wrought-iron glass-topped table, or to sit and watch the changing
shadows as the sun plays on cacti and ornamental grasses.
Right An old corrugated iron shepherd's hut on wheels is a picturesque hideaway in
this Dorset garden – and could double up as an extra summer bedroom or outdoor office.
Painted a delicate shade of green, it also creates a backdrop for planting. It can even be
trundled around the garden when you want to ring the changes.

children If you have the space – and children who love to run and ride around – then, of course, a large area of grass at some distance from the house can be set aside for games. This is the ideal, yet in all but the largest country gardens it is simply unfeasible. Rather than have the main body of the garden strewn with toys, bikes and footballs, not to mention the accompanying skid marks, try to create features that look good in themselves and fulfil a function in the garden, as well as providing a focus for children's games. Fantasy hideouts can double as follies, providing the focal point for a vista or concealing an eyesore – look for inspiration in the local landscape and legends. A castellated tower or rustic tree house is easier on the eye than a plastic slide or Wendy house – and much more fun besides. They can often be constructed quite cheaply using found wood, leftover bricks or offcuts – materials local to your area will be cheapest and possibly free. Make quite sure the structures are safe, particularly tree houses – and remember you may need to check with local authorities about large-scale permanent structures.

Smaller play features can be conjured up in the same spirit: a simple home-made swing, even a bright wooden or plastic disc on the end of a long knotted chandler's rope, has more sculptural appeal than most shop-bought versions, and sits far more happily in country surroundings. Or what about an organic play feature grown in living willow? Simple bowers and tunnels can be created by sticking coppiced willow wands in the soil (do this between November and March, when they are bare) and weaving between them in a basketwork pattern. You could attend a course or look at specialist books for instructions and ideas.

All the family enjoy garden buildings for eating in, playing in, working in or even sleeping in. They needn't be complicated or expensive.

Main picture and above left This Dutch country garden's summerhouse is a clever adaptation of a garden shed, with open windows and plants ranged along the ledges. A plain white interior and simple wooden furniture complement the straightforward timber structure and fresh, unaffected colours.

Above right Tree houses keep older children happy for hours. A sturdy platform with a ladder up into the trees may be all that is needed, with some sort of retaining fence for safety. Make sure your tree house is structurally sound, and will not harm the tree in which it sits.

Left This miniature house, with its own fence and front garden, is a decorative part of an eccentric garden. Pretty hideaways can double as follies, or be the focus for a garden vista.

Kids can join in the construction work, and the completed structure looks even more beautiful in spring when the uprights sprout into leaf, creating privacy and mystery within.

Children don't stay young for long, so consider installing or making play features that can change or be converted as they grow. A sandpit sunk in a wooden deck or stone terrace could become a pond in future years, or vice versa. A hideout could end its days as a potting shed, and the site for a swing could become a pretty hanging seat in the shade of a tree. If you have toddlers and younger children, you'll probably want to focus their play around the house, contained by a temporary stake, rope or woven willow fence. When they are older, treat them to a secret adventure playground, screened from the house by swishing bamboo, with ropes, swings and trapezes hanging from branches or sturdy scaffold frames, and a thick mulch of bark chippings on the ground to break any falls.

Right Swings can be enjoyed by people of all ages – even if the view is not quite as spectacular as this one. Children adore swings but they are also peaceful places for adults to sit and think or read a book. The simplest designs are often the most fun, and sit most happily within a country-style garden.

Above A section of found timber tied with a knot works almost like a piece of sculpture in this woodland garden, and does not detract from the rustic fence just behind it.

Left Plain sturdy constructions of wood and rope look better than plastic, with perhaps a trapeze bar at a different height for the more adventurous.

Far left Don't just stop at wood. Here, an old tin grape-treading vat has been suspended from a tree to make a safe swing for a baby.

Right You can never have too many seats dotted around the garden. Make sure some are under cover, to ensure shelter from both hot sun and rain showers. Surveying a wet garden when you are warm and dry, but close enough to see and hear the raindrops on leaves, is an unexpected joy that is only possible if you have such a place to go. Unless you are particularly prone to solitary musings in the garden, provide seats wide enough for two.
Below A matching set of woven wicker chairs makes a lawn into a sociable gathering place.

outdoor eating It makes sense to create an eating area near the house, on a deck or terrace where you can carry things in and out with ease. Sometimes the nicest furniture is the simplest – an old slab of marble or slate on stone supports, or an ancient wooden table, bleached and worn by the weather. For seats, consider simple chunks of wood, which have the graphic, year-round appeal of sculpture, or cheerfully mismatched cricket chairs. If you like to cook outside, why not design your perfect barbecue, with room to warm plates and chop vegetables alongside? For real luxury everyone will love, build a pizza oven into a wall.

One of the joys of living in the country is the pleasure of the seasons and their ever-changing views.

Right A stone shelter for animals in this former farmyard has become a splendid summer sitting and dining room. The roof provides shade and shelter, while the open sides afford uninterrupted views of the garden. The elegant metal-frame chairs are comfortable and smart, while a lazy hammock swings nearby.

Far right Weathered old furniture has the advantage that it can be left outside all year. These old French balloon chairs look wonderfully sculptural against the grass, and would quickly become comfortable with the addition of cushions. A flowerpot sunk into the table can change with the seasons.

A table under a favourite tree makes a perfect place for a family lunch or supper – somehow, home-made food tastes better outdoors. Round tables accommodate large numbers with ease, and an attractive mismatch of old chairs means that more can be added without upsetting the balance. The soft, worn colours of the paint on these folding chairs makes them less intrusive than a brand new set in bright shiny metal or plastic. Meal times apart, this lawn is the domain of the resident goats, who keep it clipped as well as contributing a friendly animal presence to the garden.

Right A herb garden can be a pleasant place to sit as well as the source of useful culinary ingredients. Herb gardens are traditionally walled or contained spaces, where different herbs are planted in a decorative pattern of beds and paths. On sunny days, the scent of the plants becomes concentrated within the garden – the effect can be quite exhilarating.

Above Raised beds are an attractive, effective way of growing organic vegetables in limited spaces. You can tend and harvest the crop without treading on, and compacting, the soil. Add a thick layer of garden compost or well-rotted manure every year. Here, the gardener has made the plot look good, with neat canes for runner beans and decorative vegetable varieties like crimson-flowered broad beans.

At times it is lovely to lay an impromptu lunch or supper elsewhere in the garden – a trestle table or two covered in white cloths and some simple folding chairs are easy to transport to where the apple trees are in blossom, or the all-too-brief roses can be admired. Create an enchanting festive bower, suspending a simple canvas awning from a tree to make extra shade at lunch time, or stretching white fairy lights between the branches at night. Lay flowers on the table and spread blankets on the ground for pets and children. The pilgrimage across the garden – everyone bearing plates and baskets and good things to eat – can form part of the fun.

Above Herbs and vegetables grow among the topiary shapes in this attractive Dutch potager. The clipped evergreen hedges and shapes are a decorative reminder that vegetables were traditionally grown within hedged beds to give shelter from harsh winds.
Above right Functional features should always be decorative in the new country garden. The shelter for chickens in this Dorset garden is a simple amalgamation of old timber, twigs and chicken wire, yet it is as attractive as a rustic summerhouse or piece of sculpture. The hens enjoy it too. Their manure is a valuable source of nutrients, and can be layered into the compost heap. If you have an orchard, let your chickens run beneath the trees, where they will improve fertility, control the grass and minimize pest problems.

vegetable gardens Eating outside is even better if you are enjoying produce raised and picked in your own garden. These days, the cheapest and best organic fruit and vegetables are those you grow yourself, and for many people this is part of the appeal of living in the country. Rather than hiding your kitchen garden away at the bottom of the garden, as is often the custom, make it a feature you are proud of. There are few things as attractive as a French-style potager, with flowers and vegetables growing together in a network

Below A fence of woven coppiced wood creates a beautiful boundary for this vegetable plot, while an additional covering of chicken wire should keep out rabbits. A twiggy arch at the far end supports scented sweet peas for picking. Smart standard bay trees with plaited trunks stand sentinel at the gate.

of neat paths and beds. But even if you opt for a more functional design using raised beds or simple rows, you can make your plot as pretty as possible. Surround it with clipped hedges or woven willow fences, and make sculptural beanpoles and plant supports from coppiced hazel twigs. For your own health, and that of the birds and bees that visit your garden, avoid chemical fertilizers and pest controls. Use beer traps for slugs and snails, and investigate biological controls for other unwelcome guests. Growing flowers among the crops can help control the damage – for example, pot marigolds and the poached egg plant

Far left and below This Dutch vegetable garden is as attractive as it is useful. A clipped arch in the surrounding hedge frames a network of cobbled paths and neat beds, where giants such as globe artichokes tower. Through the gate (left), lime-green curly endive and red oak leaf lettuce, interspersed in geometric beds, add to the display. Terracotta cloches, for forcing chicory and endive, provide height and interest all year round.

Left There is something endlessly satisfying about neat rows of cabbages, carrots and lettuces, interspersed with trussed-up bamboo canes and teepees for climbing beans. The individual leaves can be stunning, too. Take time to appreciate them, as you move among the beds to weed and harvest crops. The heavily veined leaves of the cabbage family (brassicas) are particularly beautiful, and come in a wonderful variety of shades, from pale glaucous grey-green to pink and purple and almost blue.

(*Limnanthes douglasii*) attract hoverflies, whose larvae feed on aphids, while elder and nasturtiums lure blackfly away from other plants. Attracting insects into your vegetable plot will also aid pollination, leading to higher yields.

Should you have neither the time nor the inclination to grow vegetables, it is well worth planting a few fruit trees. The blossom will be beautiful in spring, especially if it is underplanted with tiny daffodils, grape hyacinths or fritillaries, and the fruit is undemanding if you choose your varieties well. Buy from a good nursery which can advise you. Soft fruits such as strawberries and raspberries are also relatively easy and hugely rewarding, but you'll need to construct a fruit cage from chicken wire or plastic netting, or birds will get the cream of the crop. Pop in some black-, red- and white currants and you have the ingredients for the perfect summer pudding. What better end to a family lunch in the garden?

Country-style gardens have a wild edge to them. Concern for the environment, coupled with the new fashion for naturalistic planting, has led to a revival in wildlife gardening – from sowing your own wildflower meadow to planting a few bushes to encourage butterflies.

wildlife gardens

'Wildlife' gardens and flower meadows have become fashionable in recent years, but as intensive farming methods make fields and hedgerows less hospitable to birds and animals, there is also a real need to make room for wildlife in the garden. Obviously there will be some animals you won't want to welcome, but with a little extra thought and effort, plants, people and a variety of wild creatures can live happily side by side. Deer and wild rabbits are the bane of many country gardeners' lives, and if they went unchecked there would be no gardens at all. So in many areas stout fencing (with at least a foot underground and bent out at right angles to deter tunnelling rabbits) is a crucial starting point. You'll also need to protect seedlings and vulnerable plants from the

Right Clouds of cow parsley (*Anthriscus sylvestris*) billow under the young leaves of a horse chestnut tree in this wonderful Dorset garden. Known as Queen Anne's lace and lady's lace, its foaming white flowers transform British roadsides in spring. In a garden setting, cow parsley works well under trees, where it conceals the dying foliage of spring bulbs. Indoors, the flowers look good in huge bunches.

Right and far right Set on a hill above open farmland, the outer reaches of this Wiltshire garden have been designed to blend with views of the agricultural landscape. Further from the house, the mown lawn narrows to a path between long grass and wild flowers, leading to a secret seat where you can sit and admire the prospect.

Opposite page Rampant coarse grasses will usually end up dominating if land is just left to 'go native', though cow parsley and buttercups will usually rise above the competition, and don't be afraid of common daisies (*Bellis perennis*) for your lawn. You may want to encourage the more delicate wild flowers such as ox-eye or moon daisies (*Leucanthemum vulgare*) and corn chamomile (*Anthemis arvensis*), bottom right and far right, and papery field poppies (*Papaver rhoeas*), top right. In order to do this, you may have to remove the normally rich garden topsoil (keep it for other purposes) and sow seed on the poor dusty soil beneath – you can buy mixtures of wildflower seed that have been selected for particular conditions.

ravages of slugs and snails. But gardening with nature in mind means being aware of the interconnectedness of all life: there is no use in encouraging birds and toads into your garden if you sprinkle poisonous slug pellets on your potatoes.

Organic growing methods are the best foundations for a successful wildlife garden – well-rotted manure and garden compost will create a healthier soil, teeming with tiny beneficial life forms, than any artificial fertilizers. And natural pest controls, from old-fashioned beer traps sunk in the soil to catch slugs and snails, to nematodes (microscopic organisms) that are watered into the soil or released onto affected plants, are always preferable to chemical sprays that may harm beneficial creatures as well. A well-established wildlife garden should become a miniature ecosystem in itself, with pest control a naturally occurring part of the food chain – thrushes eating snails, for instance, and ladybird larvae feasting on aphids. It may take time to arrive at this ideal state of affairs, though, so be patient. And in the meantime, why not try to encourage a hedgehog or two into your garden? They love eating slugs. Or how about keeping some ducks? One of the founders of Permaculture, a school of organic gardening that aims to create a sustainable, self-perpetuating garden system, using available resources rather than buying in anything from outside, preferred to think of a 'slug problem' as 'a shortage of ducks'.

Right above A mixture of wild and cultivated plants works well around the borders of this Dorset garden, where the domestic landscape merges with wild fields and woods beyond. Choose your plants carefully – if you select varieties with small delicate flowers that still resemble their wild ancestors, you shouldn't create any unfortunate clashes. Send a rambling rose up into a tree, as here, for a tumbling shower of blooms in summer – after a little initial training up the trunk it should soon take off. These white flowers and their naturalistic growth habit complement the wild daisies in the meadow.

Right below In the same vein, the thistle-like heads of sea hollies (eryngiums) look at home among naturalistic plantings of grasses and wild flowers.

Right Sometimes the simplest effects are best. Mowing a curved path through long grass claims this area as garden, but retains a feeling of wildness. *Philadelphus* (mock orange) looks good among naturalistic plantings. The long grass obscures the end of the path, creating a welcome air of mystery.

The best way to encourage a wide range of wildlife into your garden is to create a variety of distinct habitats. Ponds, wetland areas and wildflower meadows will each provide homes for particular creatures, while specific trees and bushes attract different birds and butterflies. If you create only one wildlife feature in your garden, a pond will be the most welcome and will soon be buzzing with life. Site it in a sunny area, and make it as large as is feasibly possible – you won't regret it. Unless you have a heavy soil and can 'puddle' the bottom with a layer of natural clay, you will need to use an artificial liner, but turf laid right up to the edges, with a few rocks and stones on the banks, will soon look natural. Make sure the base of the pond is stepped or shallow-sloping on one side, so that creatures such as frogs and toads can hop in and out with ease. They, too, are great devourers of slugs and other pests, and should fill your pond with spawn every

Left Strongly shaped flower heads
stand out among the delicate
flowers and seed-heads of wild
flowers and grasses. In a stunning
piece of planting, a small orchard
of ornamental and fruit trees in
this Wiltshire garden has been
underplanted with cow parsley
and alliums. The starry spheres
of *Allium* 'Purple Sensation' are
exactly the same pinky mauve
as the blossoms on the bare
branches of the Judas tree
(*Cercis siliquastrum*) behind.
Above and right Other alliums
(above) and monardas (right) would
also look good here, and attract
pollinating bees to the fruit trees.

spring. Remember to put in oxygenating weeds
and aim to cover about a third of the surface in
plants with floating leaves, to provide shade and
help prevent algae growth. It is extraordinary how
quickly a new pond, filled with tap water, attracts
wildlife. Adding a jar of water from a neighbour's
pond will speed up the process still further. In
days you'll see water-boatmen skimming the
surface and water snails attached to plants;
newts, dragonflies and damselflies will not be
slow to follow. Lay a small branch from one side
to the other on which birds can perch to drink or
preen their feathers in the water.

The borders of your pond can be broadened
quite easily to make a marshy or wetland habitat.
Extend the lining at a depth of twenty centimetres
(eight inches) or so to one side, and fill it with soil.
Plant this area with moisture-loving plants such as
lady's smock (*Cardamine pratensis*), flag iris and
creeping jenny (*Lysimachia nummularia*), to provide
shade and feeding areas for various creatures.

Try to free your garden from the tyranny of
the lawn. A smooth green lawn may be a great
garden tradition – and good for a game of
croquet – but ecologically it's a desert. Mown
short and doused with chemicals to kill off
'weeds' (which are often native species), lawns
have little to offer insects and other wildlife, while
constant mowing and sprinkling in summer use
up precious fuel and water resources. You may
want to keep a lawn as part of your garden,
particularly if you have young children or like
to play ball games. But try letting one of the
borders, or the side that butts onto a wood
or wilder area, go 'native' and uncut for one

Right The pink moss rose
'William Lobb' is great for
naturalistic plantings as it
has a wild-looking habit but
does lend itself to training.

Far right Purple toadflax,
Linaria purpurea, is an
extremely pretty perennial
with violet-tinged flowers.
It needs good soil in full sun.

summer. It makes sense to blur the boundaries into the
surrounding countryside with an area of wilder planting, and
this will be the place where many wild creatures find a home.

Creating a haven for wildlife means more than abandoning
the lawnmower, however. If you dream of your own wildflower
meadow, ablaze with poppies, corn cockle and luminescent
grasses all summer long, this requires a deceptive amount of
effort and upkeep. The crucial thing is to encourage the right
ratio of grasses, flowers and 'weeds'; the coarser grasses in the
average lawn will choke the more attractive delicate plants you
want to encourage. Poor soil is the key to success, and you
may need to remove the topsoil before sowing. A sunny well-
drained site is the other main requirement. Mixtures of
wildflower seed for various conditions and types of meadow can
be bought from specialist nurseries, and should come with clear
instructions and a precise cutting regime. Persevere for the first
year, when the grass may be patchy and the flowers few and far
between – and feel free to 'cheat' by popping in some pot-
grown ox-eye daisies and cornflowers while the slower-growing

Left Astrantias prefer a rich soil and light shade; their delicate, star-like blooms are among the prettiest of garden flowers, and can be found in white and all shades of pink from shell to deepest crimson. They combine very successfully with ornamental grasses.

Below and right Many wild plants look beautiful long after their flowers have faded. Poppies have beautiful grey-blue seed-heads with a strong graphic shape which can contribute to a late summer border (right). Leaving the seed-heads is also the easiest way to ensure a repeat show of flowers next year. Papery petals and delicate grasses bring a sense of movement to the garden – they rustle and shimmer in the slightest breeze and catch every fleeting change of light. Position them where early morning or afternoon sun can shine through the fragile inflorescences (below).

Far right The plume poppy (*Macleaya cordata*) is a wonderful perennial that dies down every winter only to put on three metres or more (ten feet or more) of growth in the course of each summer. Its grey-green leaves have deeply indented outlines like a map of some nameless island, and the bleached buff seed-heads wave like feathers in the wind.

plants establish. By the second summer, your efforts should be rewarded by a heavenly haze of flowers and lots of happy bees, birds and butterflies. Mow a narrow curved path through your meadow – the simple contrast between close-cut and wild long grass is endlessly satisfying – and set a secret bench where you can sit and observe the constant comings and goings.

Just by taking care with the trees and bushes you choose, you can encourage all sorts of new creatures into your garden.

Right Even new formal-style gardens can be havens for wildlife – the secret is not to over-clip your hedges or topiary shapes, and to let a variety of flowering plants, which attract beneficial insects, grow into soft mounds. Leaving grass to grow a little longer between mowings will also make a difference – a close-mown lawn is a green desert.

Right This skilful mixture of fuzzy *Calamagrostis brachytricha* with mauve monardas and crimson *Persicaria amplexicaulis* is stunning. The grasses create a constantly shifting screen through which the other plants can be glimpsed.

Right The seed-heads of ornamental grasses such as *Panicum virgatum* are not only beautiful, they are also a boon for the birds, who will enjoy perching on them and pecking at the seeds through the winter. Most varieties don't need cutting back until February or March.

Butterflies need particular host plants among which to live and breed, as well as nectar-rich feeding plants like red valerian and buddleia – all attractive in themselves. Any large tree will invite hundreds of birds and insects, but if you are selecting young trees, think about berries for the birds in autumn – a rowan (*Sorbus aucuparia*), crab apple (*Malus*) or hawthorn (*Crataegus monogyna*). Missel thrushes and blackbirds like red or orange berries. Nail nesting boxes in sheltered places, and in winter, hang feeders where cats and squirrels can't intrude. A free-standing bird table in view of the house is a great joy all year.

Right A wildflower meadow is not only a wonderful addition to your garden, it is a welcome contribution to the wider landscape, providing a habitat for insects and indigenous creatures, including many whose homes in the wild are under threat from new housing or chemical farming methods. All summer long, the froth of flowers will be quivering with insects and butterflies and humming with life.

Above *Pennisetum alopecuroides* has fuzzy seed-heads which catch the light in an incandescent halo on late summer afternoons.

PART TWO

elements

designing the garden

grassy paths and stone steps

hedges from tamed to overblown

natural woven willow

garden features

framing the view

original containers and plant supports

organic garden art

water features

tranquil reflections and mesmerizing movement

sunken ponds and garden pools

perfect plants

giants in the border

accent plants and distracting details

a colour gallery

Left, above and right
Woven fences in coppiced wood define different areas in this modern rural garden in Holland. Using natural local materials in a simple yet stylish design is the essence of the new country look. Woven fencing panels can be bought ready-made, but it is fun and easy to make your own – they keep out the wind while allowing some air to circulate. The moss growing on the fences and picket gate adds to their natural beauty.

The division of space in a garden into different areas with distinct uses and atmospheres is the essence of garden design. But walls, fences and paths are more than mere boundary markers. They can become attractive garden features in their own right when fashioned creatively from local materials.

designing the garden

All gardens are designed, to a greater or lesser extent. A well-planned garden shouldn't make you think immediately, 'What a well-designed garden!' It should simply feel like a wonderful place in which to be. However, a badly designed space will seem wrong from the start. Nothing will be where you need it, and its features will be uneasy on the eye. Good garden design may seem elusive, but it is the vital ingredient whereby the various elements of the garden – plants, hard surfaces, practical and aesthetic features – are integrated into a pleasing and well-functioning whole.

before you start Few people have the opportunity, or the budget, to design a garden from scratch. Most of us have to integrate our own ideas within a framework laid out by

somebody else, and a degree of compromise may be necessary. If you have a large area to cope with, or have a particularly special feature in mind, it may be a good idea to employ a professional garden designer. Many designers now work on a consultancy basis, where they will charge for an initial visit and a scaled-up drawing of the new design, which can then be given to your own builder or contractor. This can cost less than having the designer oversee the whole process – but, either way, you shouldn't have cause to regret the extra money spent. If you do use a professional garden designer, as a consultant or for the whole project, remember that much of the initial visit will be spent talking – about who uses the garden, how you use it, whether there are particular features, such as

Above Promoting a formal look, stone balls flank an opening in this huge copper beech hedge in Ireland. The dark foliage creates the perfect foil for the white house beyond, where more stone balls and standard bay trees in pots provide a unifying link in the composition. The woolly growth above will eventually be clipped to follow the arch.

Left A rustic wooden arch surrounded by dense foliage frames a view of a more distant arch – this time just a couple of branches sunk in the soil. Each opening marks a further progression into the wilder landscape beyond the garden.

Opposite Pleached hornbeams form a sort of hedge on stilts, creating a shady allée beside an area of exuberant planting in this Scottish garden. Young trees were planted close together and carefully pruned and trained as they grew, until the upper sections fused to form a solid strip of foliage. The rest of the garden can be glimpsed between the tree trunks, which throw striped shadows across the grassy path. Limes and beeches can also be grown in this way.

Above Curved paths and hedges are a graceful way of creating mystery in the garden. As the path sweeps slowly round, the final destination is kept hidden until the last minute. The higher the hedge, the greater the degree of secrecy and privacy attained, of course. The low hedge above has rugosa roses growing in it, a pretty touch well suited to this Dutch family garden.

Right Keeping the grass close-mown around the edges of the lawn in this Dutch garden creates a path from which the border can be admired. The area around the swing has been kept short too – the rest is left long for the goats. Woven wood fences are necessary to stop the livestock penetrating the formal gardens. The younger trees also have protective baskets around their trunks.

water or a summerhouse, that you want to include, and how much maintenance you want to do. Sitting down and talking to others who use the garden is an excellent starting point for planning changes. Try to sit in the garden, or at least in an open doorway, and make notes and sketches of your ideas as you go.

This is not the place to go into detail about the process and principles of designing a garden. There are many specialist books available to guide you on this particular subject, and many of your decisions will be dependent upon the type and size of space you have and how you want to use it. (See *Garden Features* on page 96 for ideas on relating the house to the landscape.) You may want to include any or all of the following: a terraced area outside the house, a lawn for lying or playing games on, large areas of naturalistic planting, a formal rose or herb garden, a swimming pool, a vegetable plot, a wildflower meadow or a woodland garden. What is certain is that you will need to divide up the space into different areas – usually by means of fences, walls or hedges – and link them by paths, steps or other features. There are always obvious and more imaginative options when planning and constructing such vital garden elements. Give the matter just a little more thought, and you will be able to come up with the materials and methods that are right for your style of garden.

Right In this courtyard garden in Wiltshire, the curved section of hedge is yew (*Taxus baccata*), and forms a dense-growing, deep green backdrop for the plants growing on the other side. The lawn has been mown in neat stripes to follow the curve of the hedge.

Below and right The charm and atmosphere of this Luxembourg garden hinge on its radiating hedged allées, like green corridors, that invite visitors in different directions. The grass paths are mown frequently to contrast with the leafiness elsewhere. The state of the hedges determines the mood: clipped close, they create a modern formal garden, a restrained symphony of greens; left to grow longer, their shagginess makes a mysterious, fairy-tale quality.

dividing space All the elements of the new country garden must be in harmony with one another, and suited to its relaxed and creative style. Hedges, walls and fences have their practical purposes, of course – to keep animals and humans in or out, act as a shelter or screen for plants or people, and as a support for climbing or scrambling plants. But they also help to set the house in its surroundings, and create a textured yet regular backdrop for the plants that grow against them. Materials that have some relevance to the house and its nearby landscape are likely to be more successful on all levels. Historically, people have always used local materials for building: wood in forested areas; brick where there is clay; slate, flint and

Right Chunky low box hedges define the borders of this paved pool garden in Ireland and help preserve the still, quiet atmosphere created by water. Box's dense habit lends itself to graphic shapes – here cubist hedges and cones contrast beautifully with other foliage in the garden beyond. The containers can be moved around; plain glazed pots or galvanized bins would give a more modern look.

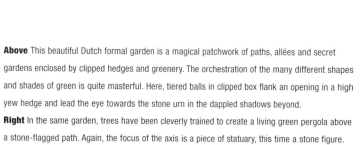

Above This beautiful Dutch formal garden is a magical patchwork of paths, allées and secret gardens enclosed by clipped hedges and greenery. The orchestration of the many different shapes and shades of green is quite masterful. Here, tiered balls in clipped box flank an opening in a high yew hedge and lead the eye towards the stone urn in the dappled shadows beyond.

Right In the same garden, trees have been cleverly trained to create a living green pergola above a stone-flagged path. Again, the focus of the axis is a piece of statuary, this time a stone figure.

dry stone wherever they are plentiful. If you are lucky enough to have an old wall or well-established hedge in your garden, do keep it – and take care of it by repairing it with similar materials.

But don't be afraid of the new. People have always added new elements to houses and gardens through the centuries, and there is a satisfying honesty about new vernacular materials, properly placed and skilfully crafted. Stone or brick walls give a garden a sense of solidity and permanence and, if they are high enough, of privacy too. Walls of dry stone, red brick, knapped flint or concrete provide different backdrops up which plants can grow – try to match the right colours and textures with the right materials – and a south-facing wall, which retains a lot of heat, makes an ideal habitat for fruit trees or slightly tender plants. Retaining walls can be used to create terraces on sloping ground, sometimes with raised beds in which plants can cascade down a hillside, and steps leading up and down. All walls require concrete foundations, so consult a do-it-yourself manual for details if you want to build your own.

Fences are less durable than walls, but they hold endless creative possibilities. If intruders are not a problem, old-fashioned stake fences, or a simple post-and-rail barrier in local wood, are attractive and allow virtually uninterrupted views of the surrounding landscape. More solid fences – woven

Above The leaves of this zigzag beech hedge will turn a beautiful rustling copper in autumn, and lend a 'see-through' quality to the winter garden. Strong lines such as this work well in conjunction with architecture, and must be trimmed frequently to retain their sharp graphic shapes. The enclosing V shapes of the zigzag create sheltered settings for plants on either side.

Right Shallow stone steps and a wide gravel path invite exploration of the wilder, naturalistic part of the garden beyond the hedge, while the formal gardens are hidden behind the brick wall on the right. Lavender always looks good spilling onto paths and steps and softens the hard lines and materials.

Centre right A shady corridor linking areas of this Californian garden has been transformed into a feature in its own right, by painting the walls and choosing plants that thrive in these conditions. Climbers are starting to cover the wall, while the palm tree fronds create an archway into the space beyond.

Far right Local stone has been used to make modern dry stone walls in this stylish contemporary garden around a converted Wiltshire barn.

Above Scalloping the edges of the grass border to this gravel drive in Herefordshire is a simple but effective way to create a dramatic approach to the house.

Right Willow fences and hurdle panels are useful ways to divide off areas of the garden while still letting through some light and air – and some glimpses of the plants within. Modern yet rustic, they fit well into contemporary vegetable gardens. Home-made versions such as this have an unpredictable charm.

willows or hurdles, for instance – will act as windbreaks, but can be constructed with strategic gaps or windows to frame views in and out. Willow is ideal for the new country garden. Although it is a traditional technique, woven willow looks fresh and contemporary, and it can be woven in a variety of patterns and styles, from simple basketwork to more complex scalloped edges and spiky finials. You can buy hurdle panels ready made, but why not attend a course to learn how to make them? Or, for a smart modern take on tradition, try painting a picket fence an unusual colour, such as grey or purple. Leave larger than usual gaps between posts so that fragrant plants like lavender and herbs can spill out and release their scent as people brush past. Trellis can work well on top of a solid fence, to provide extra privacy and support for climbing plants while still allowing air and light through. Forget the flimsy stuff of garden centres and construct chunky custom-built panels from lengths of wood or large bamboo – you can either paint them or let them weather naturally. A trellis panel attached to a deep wooden planter at the base can be moved around the garden like a portable screen.

Steps are a useful way of connecting different levels in the garden, and can themselves be attractive features. **Right** Brick weathers well and quickly. These semi-circular steps, like tiers on a wedding cake, lead from one area of lawn to another. Plants' organic shapes soften the lines of hard landscaping; here, lady's mantle (*Alchemilla mollis*) has self-seeded in the mortar. **Opposite left** The impressive reclaimed Georgian stone arch requires a suitably grand approach, and these stone steps, flanked by box hedges and guarded by clipped balls in pots, are elegant yet unpretentious. **Opposite right** Timber can also make steps. Here, salvaged railway sleepers contain gravel in which sun-loving echeverias and evening primroses are thriving. **Below** Stone flags are timeless and romantic, and weather attractively. Wide, shallow treads leave room for self-seeding plants like the pretty daisy *Erigeron karvinskianus* to gather in cracks and spill over edges.

Hedges make excellent living boundaries and divisions in the new country garden, providing shelter from winds and strong seasonal interest. Mixed-species hedges provide blossom and changing foliage throughout the year, and are a good way to encourage wildlife into the garden, as they offer the variety of nesting sites and food sources that is fast disappearing from the wild. Oak, holly, hawthorn and *Rosa rugosa* might find a place in such a hedge, perhaps with honeysuckle, ivy or clematis twining among them. For a more formal look, grow single-species hedges of box, beech or yew in well-prepared trenches. Plant in staggered double rows for a wider hedge. Bear in mind that you may need to provide a windbreak while the seedlings establish. With certain types of hedging – hawthorn and beech among them – you can allow some of the hedging plants to grow unchecked into trees, or make arches over gates or paths.

Above and right A well-chosen collection of chairs animates a garden and immediately identifies it as a relaxed and sociable place. Even when there is no one sitting on them, these attractive, mismatched old folding chairs, metal balloon chairs and slatted cricket seats create a pleasing picture in the garden, and recall long summer lunches and candlelit parties.

Rustic needn't mean retro when it comes to garden features. Modern ideas and unusual materials look just as at home in a country-style garden as in a town one, bringing a contemporary edge to traditional seats, gazebos and plant supports, and blurring the boundaries between arts and crafts.

garden features

No matter how beautiful, a garden that relies purely on plants will lack focus. Seats, summerhouses and sculpture – even plants themselves trimmed into shapes or trained in unusual ways – can be used to lead the eye around the garden, creating areas of intimacy and intrigue and inviting exploration. All garden features, from permanent structures to the smallest seats or plant supports, must be incorporated carefully into the overall design. Good looks alone are not enough: unless the pieces are thoughtfully placed, they will look as if they have landed by parachute. The crucial thing is to avoid the fiddly and fussy. New country style favours strong simple shapes and honest materials.

Below The intense colour of the beautiful double *Delphinium* 'Alice Artindale' makes it a feature in itself. Delphiniums are available in all shades of blue and purple, from white and pale mauves through glorious two-tone effects to deepest indigo.

Left One of a pair of curved seats placed so one can enjoy an enclosed area of this Dorset garden, which is devoted to dramatic 'Venetian' colours – deep purples and blues and rich reds and crimsons that glow with all the sombre splendour of the velvet draperies in some grand Venetian portrait. The bench resembles antique stone but is in fact cast concrete bought from a local garden centre and weathered – a mixture of soil, water and yogurt accelerates the process.

framing the view Sometimes a garden needs a feature to terminate a vista – to provide the visual focus at the end of an allée of pleached limes, for instance, or to inhabit a woodland glade. If you are thinking of a seat or summerhouse for this purpose, ensure the view in the other direction is similarly attractive, and that the site receives some sun at a useful time of day. If not, a piece of sculpture might sit more happily. At other times it is a matter of fitting a desired feature – a sundial or gazebo, for example – into an existing design.

Be aware of the effect that such features have on visitors: they force them to slow down and linger. A seat will obviously invite a longer stay – and if there is another view to be seen on a different axis, placing the seat at right angles will allow visitors to appreciate it before resuming their route around the garden.

Gateways and arbours that frame a view also help to pace the visitor and alert them to the effects of your handiwork. They were used in this way by the grand landscape gardeners of the eighteenth century, but where they would have used a grandiose arch or urn, go for something quieter. Even a pair of simple bare branches, sunk in the ground and crossed overhead to make an impromptu arch will have the effect of saying: 'Stop. Look. See what is here.' Such gateways can also mark the progression from one section of the garden to another, prompting a recognition of the change on both a physical and an emotional level. Different areas can have sharply differing moods, and well-considered sculptures and other features can help prepare for and reflect the changes, or weave a theme – such as death and rebirth, or a particular colour – like a thread throughout the garden.

Right This simply decorated wooden bench is as beautiful as a piece of sculpture. Set in the shade of trees, it affords a view of the summerhouse across the lawn.

Far right Hammocks have a wonderful air of laziness and decadence. This cream canvas one is slung on sturdy hooks across the entrance to a former barn – perfectly positioned so the person lying on it can enjoy the scent of the roses climbing up the wall.

Left Evergreens clipped into drums, cones, cubes and other simple shapes are as closely packed as chess pieces in this Dutch garden.

Right A hedge of box has been skilfully trained up around and in front of a stone bench to create this witty seat.

Far right Box has been clipped to create a chunky sweeping curve that embraces the enclosed space like a protective arm.

Below Topiary can lend an air of mystery to a garden, particularly if the shapes have been allowed to become slightly overgrown. The truncated column adds to the romantic atmosphere.

topiary As well as considering static garden features, remember that plants themselves can be transformed into living sculpture. Topiary is often thought of as part of the old-style formal garden, but it has been undergoing a renaissance in recent years as a new generation of gardeners discovers its strong graphic potential. The key to contemporary topiary is to keep the shapes simple: cubes, cones or close-clipped mounds look best, while the impact of a row of holly, bay or box trees clipped as 'lollipop' standards is indisputable. As well as the traditional candidates for topiary, consider more unusual possibilities: Kilmarnock willows (*Salix caprea* 'Kilmarnock') trimmed into silvery grey mushrooms; winter-flowering *Viburnum tinus* as a fragrant cube; or even gooseberries, redcurrants and blackcurrants as container-grown standards. Topiary has always had a humorous edge, but modern gardeners forgo the giant green teapots and chickens of yesterday in favour of a less obvious approach. Modern topiary relies on strong graphic shapes and subtle visual jokes for impact: leave fiddly figures and comic animals to traditionalists. Close-textured plants such as box can be clipped into living garden furniture,

Arches and bowers can frame a view, create welcome shade and shelter, and support a variety of beautiful climbing plants. They can also mark the progression from one area of the garden to another, making the visitor slow down and become aware of a change in theme or atmosphere.

Right The nearest bower is totally obscured by leafy vines, while the climbing roses scrambling up the far one leave some of the structure visible – both are attractive.

Far right A series of wide, well-spaced metal arches has been placed to frame the view of the tree beyond and lead the eye out over the countryside. Honeysuckles, clematis and the chocolate-flowered vine, *Akebia quinata*, are being trained up the supports, but it looks quite dramatic left bare.

for instance, while rows of 'mop-head' standards can grow out of a series of green cubes that read as 'pots'. Sometimes the sheer number and proximity of topiarized plants provides the humour – a jumble of shapes and sizes crowded into an outdoor 'room' like guests at a cocktail party. There is no doubt that plants trained and trimmed in this way take on a mysterious life of their own.

art in the garden An important development in contemporary gardens is the lessening of the old divisions between art and the traditional crafts. A woven willow fence may march round the periphery of a garden like a Giacometti sculpture; rough-hewn blocks of wood may have the appeal of an Anthony Caro but work just as well as seats; a line of bright plant supports, devoid of foliage in winter, can have the impact of a gallery installation. This sort of

sculpture is a world away from the stone figures and cast concrete on sale in many garden centres. Look to young modern artists for minimalist, pared-down shapes in stone, wood or metal, or consider local stone carvers or blacksmiths who work with materials gleaned from the surrounding landscape. Or you could commission someone to create a work of art for a specific site. This can become an exciting collaboration, and if you choose an up-and-coming artist you could end up with an affordable one-off piece that might become a collector's item. If you are short on space, think of ways in which a sculpture could double up as a seat, a shelter, or even a bird bath. If you have access to a stone carver, a simple inscription – a fragment of a poem or just a single word – can imbue your piece's surroundings with talismanic power.

Left Simple arcs of supple coppiced wood make a splendidly irregular support for sweet peas in this contemporary cutting garden. Such features are easy to make and bring an element of wit and spontaneity to the new country garden.

Right A crenellated top transforms this Gothic bridge over a stream into something a little more grand, and lends a fairy-tale feel to the garden.

Below Roses and vines are excellent choices for growing over arches. In this Dutch garden, a series of metal frames creates a floral tunnel leading from one area to another. The arches will trap the scent of the roses in the summer, making walking beneath them a deliciously sensual experience.

Left Sometimes, you can try too hard when creating features for the garden. After all, what could be more effective, and more suitable, to mark the entrance to this Dorset wildflower meadow than this simplest of wooden arches? A pair of bent branches has been stuck into the soil, almost as if a passing walker had abandoned them, to leave a rustic and fragmented echo of a Gothic arch. A pointed arch, however simple, has sacred overtones. As well as framing the view beyond, it directs the eye upwards, linking the earth with the heavens. An arch will also make visitors to the garden stop and consider for a moment what is beyond. Without this unobtrusive entrance, the overgrown path through the meadow might be overlooked.

You could even try your hand at creating your own garden art. Take inspiration from artists who work closely with nature, such as Andy Goldsworthy and Richard Long, but try to make the piece your own. Unless you are experienced, it is probably best to keep things simple: an interesting fragment of wood or stone could make a modern menhir; a length of mirror or strangely shaped piece of metal suspended from a tree can lend an air of mystery. Found objects that have been unearthed in the garden and given a new lease of life have a special power – site them where the visitor will want to pause in thought. And a very special quality takes over a garden when the features within it are fashioned from materials found on site. The English garden designer Ivan Hicks, whose work is shown on these pages, makes this approach to garden features his speciality, blurring the distinction between craft and sculpture.

Left Features do not need to be complex to be effective. Just a simple gilded or mirrored ball, placed in shallow water or somewhere else where its reflections can be seen to good effect, can transform a garden from simply a beautiful place into a setting for mystery and magic. Sometimes known as 'witches' balls', these mirrored spheres can reflect the full 360 degrees of the garden, and bounce the sunlight into otherwise gloomy corners.

Well-placed artworks designed by Ivan Hicks.
Top left A simple cairn of stones on top of an old stone frame has all the power and presence of a piece of modern art, and will weather beautifully in this woodland corner.

Left An old metal hoop from a cartwheel, set among the branches of this ancient apple tree, frames the view out between the hedges to the fields beyond the garden boundary.

Right A pile of old flints has been rearranged into a spiral pattern, their white edges contrasting with the carpet of dark moss. Features such as these become an integral part of this Dorset garden, wedded to the site rather than brought in from outside and put down where they look right. For the visitor, walking around the garden, happening upon a series of such features is exciting, like being drawn deeper into a spell.

Left These openwork pyramids, made from coppiced hazel wands, are plant supports but have some of the sculptural appeal of a creation by the artist Andy Goldsworthy. Their geometric structure makes an interesting contrast to the wild clouds of campanulas, sedums and geraniums. This Wiltshire garden makes good use of local stone and wood, which helps to build visual and cultural links with the surrounding country.

plant containers Well-chosen containers can also create focal points. Container gardening is gaining ground, particularly in smaller gardens where space is at a premium, or on terraces just outside the house. One of its virtues is that you can move the pots into prime position, or even carry them inside the house, when they are looking at their best. When that show's over, there will be another waiting in the wings, if you aim to plant for a succession of blooms from early spring onwards. If you're clever, the container becomes an integral part of the display – there is real satisfaction in matching the right plants with the right pots. Painted wooden troughs go well with new country style, while zinc and distressed metal look good with silvery leaved plants like *Santolina*, *Helichrysum* and *Artemisia*. Traditional terracotta contrasts well with glossy evergreens, and now comes in a variety of interesting shapes and textures.

These days there's a wider than ever choice of containers on the market – but some of the most original and eye-catching are those you make yourself.

Simple wooden supports sit well in the garden, and add height and interest in winter when most plants have died down.

Above An eccentric mix of twigs and fabric strips adorns this sweet pea wigwam, the perfect foil for the wayward mixture of brightly coloured malvas and nasturtiums. Strong verticals like this act as punctuation marks among lower-growing plants.

Left Evergreen bay (*Laurus nobilis*) is being trained into an obelisk shape within this simple wooden structure. It looks good while the plant is growing, and is retained to help with pruning once the desired height and width have been reached.

Right Woven willow teepees are easy to make or can be bought in a range of sizes. Traditionally created as supports for sweet peas in old-fashioned cottage gardens, those with a contemporary twist fit well in the new country garden. The pointed shape is effective against a backdrop of white clouds of *Crambe cordifolia* and delicate white convolvulus.

Above Hanging baskets are often sneezed at by fashionable gardeners, but the secret is to choose an attractive, non-plastic basket and fill it with just one thing, not a technicolour mixture of different flowers. Here, a few strawberry plants not only look good, you can enjoy the fruit too.

Top Ranged outside the windows of this modern house in Hertfordshire, tender plants such as scented-leaf pelargoniums and the pineapple lily (*Eucomis bicolor*) are interspersed with self-seeded *Verbena bonariensis*, whose electric violet heads create a transparent purple screen. When temperatures fall in winter, the pots can be taken inside.

Above Weathered metal containers are especially appropriate for silver-leaved plants. This collection of old copper and lead planters is filled with helichrysum, alpine dianthus, *Phormium tenax* and the peacock-blue bracts of *Cerinthe major* 'Purpurascens'.

Left Bold sculptural plants such as agapanthus suit big containers, and can be moved into prime position when in bloom. When the flowers fade, let something else take their place.

Gravel on the surface of the soil in pots can look decorative. It also acts as a water-preserving and weed-suppressing mulch. It's worth investigating aquarium gravels in pet shops for unusual colours such as blue and indigo, which look great with the right coloured flowers and foliage. Old scallop or mussel shells can be used for the same purpose in a seaside garden, while mounds of moss would be stunning in damp shade. Local materials that have some sort of resonance with the surrounding landscape should always be first choice when choosing or creating garden features. Things may have changed a great deal since Sir Alexander Pope was writing and gardening in the eighteenth century, but we should still 'consult the genius of the place in all'.

Old or new dustbins, metal buckets, antique fluted laundry bins, and even old watering cans can be pressed into use and arranged in groups for the strongest effects. These one-offs add a quirky character to a garden. Whatever container you use, drainage is crucial. Too fast and the pots will dry out rapidly in summer and need watering twice a day. Too slow (the most common cause of failure) and the soil will become waterlogged, causing plants' roots to rot. If the pot or container you want to use doesn't have at least one good-sized hole in the bottom, make some with a drill. The holes should then be covered with a flat stone or shards of ceramic to stop liquid running straight out when you water. It's also a good idea to fill the base of the pot with gravel so the roots are never sitting in stagnant water. Add a small piece of charcoal to act as a filter and stop the water smelling.

Top left Terracotta pots age well – pick up old ones from junk shops and house sales. The lichen and moss that forms around the edges is part of their charm.

Left Arrange potted plants on garden furniture as you would bunches of flowers around the house. Part of the fun of container gardening is to match the pot to the plant, choosing colours, shapes and materials that suit the flowers and foliage. In this context it is also important to match the style of containers with the furniture – shiny new pots would look wrong on top of this weathered old table.

Water features in new country gardens are a far cry from the Peter Pan fountains and miniature waterfalls of the past. Shapes are simple and graphic, and materials are sleek and modern – smooth stone, polished concrete, and even glass. Narrow rills of water can lead the eye around a garden, while small fountains – even just a bamboo spout emptying into a bowl – can transform a quiet corner into a spot for meditation.

water features

Water brings sound, movement and energy to a garden as well as visual beauty. Some country gardeners may be lucky enough to have a natural water feature as part of the garden: a duck pond near the house, perhaps, or a stream running along the boundary. Make the most of them – a stream can be used to create further water features in other parts of the garden. Naturalistic brooks and wildlife ponds work well where the garden runs into the countryside, or in areas of wildflower planting. Nearer the house, take a cue from the architecture, containing the water behind stone-clad walls or trim wooden decking. A stream can become a smart minimalist rill; a mill pond a

Above Water lilies about to burst into bloom among the reflections in the pool in front of a stone portico in Ireland.
Left This still, shallow geometric pool is the culmination of a journey through a series of different spaces in this garden in the Scottish hills. Edged in stone and surrounded by severe beech hedges, it is a stunning exercise in restraint – its simplicity gives this space at the top of the garden an almost spiritual quality.

Below Still water works as a mirror, reflecting the sky or branches overhead to bring another dimension into the garden. Here in Luxembourg, the mirrored ball works particularly well in water, taking the reflections one step further.
Bottom A spray fountain brings the dynamism of moving water to this garden, shooting water into the sky and creating ever-changing patterns on the pool's surface. Visitors are always drawn to the sound of water in motion.

Left This naturalistic pool, surrounded by rocks and pebbles, is perfect for a gravel garden. Marginal plants like bulrushes, kingcups and flag irises are thriving around the edges, and sit well with the naturalistic planting in the rest of this East Anglian garden. Comfortable chairs, their wood bleached silver like driftwood, are positioned where the peaceful atmosphere that water in a garden creates can be enjoyed. Rocks and fragments of wood create hiding places for frogs and toads, as well as contributing to the beauty of the garden.

glassy pool with a single jet of water. Banish lingering images of the kidney-shaped plastic pool liners of the past. Strong graphic shapes such as squares and circles – even triangles and crescent moons – work well, especially in gardens with a 'new formal' feel.

Water is often the single most expensive item in a garden redesign, but it is guaranteed to have the most dramatic impact. Plan what you want very carefully. Consider the relationship of water to different areas and their various uses – the sound and sight of running water has an energizing effect on air quality, while still pools and quietly trickling fountains create a more soothing and tranquil atmosphere. Use large concrete stepping stones or simple slate bridges for access. Crossing even a narrow expanse of water can be a dramatic progression from one area of the garden to another: a symbolic entrance to another world.

Left This raised pool in a Californian courtyard is reminiscent of Moorish gardens – in hot climates water is appreciated for its cooling and humidifying effect on the air. The pool has been designed as an integral part of the garden, and its tiled edges are wide enough to provide extra seating if needed. The clear blue skies and exuberant, exotic planting are reflected in the pool's dark interior. Dark tiles or paint on the inside walls will increase a pool's reflective capacity, creating an effect not unlike an abstract painting on the surface.

Sculpture placed next to water seems to be imbued with extra power and meaning – or consider a kinetic sculpture, in which moving water is an integral part of the design.

One of the most beautiful aspects of using water in a country garden lies in its reflective potential – trapping the sunshine and reflecting the ever-changing patterns of clouds, flowers and foliage. The simplest shapes are best for this: a square pool, lined with stone flags and bordered by evergreen hedges, or a single circle in a wildflower lawn. Follow the example of the late designer David Hicks and paint the base of a pool

Opposite left A pond or water feature is a good opportunity to introduce moisture-loving plants to your garden. Some of them are quite spectacular, such as the giant rhubarb, *Gunnera manicata*, with its enormous umbrella-like leaves and spiky prehistoric-looking flower heads in spring. Traditionally grown on the margins of ponds and lakes, it dies down in winter; the dormant crowns will need a mulch of straw as frost protection.

Opposite right This very successful modern water feature in Wiltshire is bordered by contemporary decking on one side and bricks on the other. Flag irises do well by water, and these white ones are particularly beautiful.

Below Arum lily (*Zantedeschia aethiopica*).

Left Water features are often arranged in sequences down a hillside. In this modern take on tradition, a still round pool surrounded by hedging sits at the top of the garden, a peaceful place to look down at the rest. This secret pool is a reward for exploring countless green paths and allées.

midnight blue for more dramatic reflections; plant a border of bright flowers whose reflections will create the effect of an abstract painting shifting on the surface. At night, lighting beneath the water will throw eerily beautiful shadows of fish swimming around the walls.

Do not be put off using water for fear of its potential danger to children. Extremely dramatic effects can be achieved using only an inch or two of water. Galvanized metal grilles can be laid over water near the house when very young children are around, with no great detriment to the design – and kids will enjoy the effect of seeming to walk on water. Shallow square pools can be covered over with lockable decking 'lids' or even converted into sandpits for toddlers. Most children will delight in the wildlife visitors such as birds, frogs and toads, and dragonflies and other insects that will be attracted to well-managed water in a garden.

Above and left Attractive wild planting around a small pond in this Dutch garden, where orange Welsh poppies (*Meconopsis cambrica*) and lime-green lady's mantle (*Alchemilla mollis*) have self-seeded at the water's edge, and water lilies are about to bloom on the surface. Delphiniums on the opposite bank will echo the pale blue colour of the summerhouse in the distance.
Right This candelabra primula, *Primula beesiana*, originally from China, is a stunning plant that does well in moist ground near lakes and ponds. The 60-cm (2-ft) long flower stems hold five to seven whorls of yellow-eyed, red-purple flowers.

perfect plants

Of course, it is up to you which plants you choose for your garden. Looking at plants wherever you go and noting down those you like best is a good place to start. To give any garden that distinctive 'new country' twist, try selecting a few of your favourites from the groups described on the following pages: everything from Architectural Foliage and Giants in the Border to Accent Plants and the Tiniest Details.

Right *Echinacea purpurea* Elton Hybrids. Echinaceas look stunning from bud to bald seed-head – their strong daisy shape is useful in prairie-style planting and makes a wonderful cut flower.
Below *Helenium* 'Moerheim Beauty' has beautiful daisy-like flowers in tawny brown and orange. It is a good partner for ornamental grasses in the late summer border.

Above *Iris ensata.*
Right Aquilegias are particularly beautiful in their pure white form, as here, or in stylish modern colours such as deep wine red or the fashionable black and white 'Magpie'.

Bottom left Green flowers are always seductive, and those of the Corsican hellebore (*Helleborus argutifolius*) are particularly welcome in the depths of winter. They last well into spring.

Below Related to cow parsley, but a delightful shade of pink, *Chaerophyllum hirsutum* 'Roseum' is a fashionable addition to the new country garden, its froth of candyfloss blooms reaching 60–90 cm (2–3 ft) in early summer.

Right Even in a photograph, red tulips leap off the page as if in 3D – the effect of bright red against a green ground, which can be used for startling impact in a garden border.

Right The daisy-like flowers of *Arctotis hirsuta* (African daisy) are good for ground cover in a warm spot where you want a sudden shock of colour. Originally from South Africa, they are only half-hardy in this country, and come in rich shades of orange, yellow and pink.

Bottom right The most fashionable among dahlias, 'Bishop of Llandaff' has brilliant scarlet blooms above beautiful deep burgundy stems and leaves.

hot colours

Sizzling reds and shocking pinks are some of the most fashionable colours for today's gardens. Rather than toning them down with cooler shades and natural tones, turn up the temperature still higher by partnering them with the boldest, brightest oranges. Colours of equally strong intensity don't clash, they create a buzzing halo of energy that the eye can't leave alone. Among the best reds are the bright red yarrow, *Achillea millefolium* 'Fire King'; the scarlet dahlia 'Bishop of Llandaff', with its striking dark foliage; the deep red nasturtiums 'Empress of India' and 'Red Wonder'; the daylily *Hemerocallis* 'Aztec'; and going over into deep crimson, the rose 'Lilli Marlene', the castor oil plant, *Ricinus communis* 'Carmencita', and the rich velvety *Salpiglossis* 'Chocolate Pot'. For pinks, try oriental poppies, magenta mallows and fluffy thalictrums, while stunning oranges include the California poppy, *Eschscholzia californica*; *Lilium* 'Fire King'; and daisy-like gazanias.

Below Achilleas are useful in a mixed border, where their huge saucers of flowers contribute a strong horizontal shape. Very vigorous, they quickly form a large clump, and in strong shades such as the bright red *Achillea* 'Fanal', create a fantastic mass of colour.

Right The California poppy (*Eschscholzia californica*) self-seeds readily in poor, well-drained soil; its papery petals close up on cloudy days. A less common cream variety can also be found – the two look good growing side by side.

Above The rose 'Lilli Marlene' is one of the strongest reds of all the roses. Some other good strong reds are provided by the scarlet species rose, *Rosa moyesii* 'Geranium', the crimson Gallica rose, 'Tuscany Superb', the climbing roses 'Ena Harkness' and 'Cramoisi Supérieur', and the beautiful old Hybrid Perpetual 'Souvenir du Docteur Jamain', whose stunning deep crimson blooms prefer to be out of direct sunlight.

Opposite left *Salvia sclarea* var. *turkestanica*, commonly known as clary sage, is an extremely useful plant for the new country border. Though it is a traditional cottage garden plant, its tall spires of pink-flecked petals and bracts have a strong architectural quality and look fantastic when dried in winter. In full bloom, it combines a dramatic size and shape with beautiful filigree detail – a painter could make intricate watercolour studies of the pink stems and pointed pastel flowers. It grows up to 1.5 m (5 ft) tall and makes a bulky candelabrum shape. The plant smells strongly when touched; though some people find its fragrance disagreeable, its essential oil is used in aromatherapy preparations.

Below The double form of the white peony *Paeonia lactiflora* has stunning pompom heads in late May.

Top left The white opium poppy (*Papaver somniferum*) looks beautiful shimmering in twilight.

Top right The flowers of *Astrantia major* form a neat ruff of petals around a central pincushion. Until recently, astrantias were sadly underrated garden plants, but they are now more widely used, particularly in 'new perennial' planting schemes, where their delicate, starry flowers in subtle shades of white and pink shine out among the foliage of other plants. They are moisture-loving plants, suitable for light woodland, though the darker colours do not show up well in shade.

Above Commonly known as the Himalayan poppy, *Meconopsis betonicifolia* has startling bright blue flowers. It prefers rich acid woodland conditions.

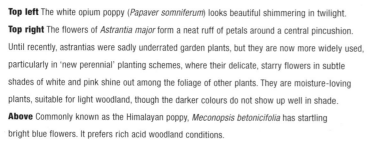

Below right *Campanula*
'Burghaltii' is one of the
many stunning campanulas
in subtle shades from white
and speckled pink through
to crimson. The palest
colours look good against
a dark backdrop, where
they light up like lanterns
when light begins to fade.

cool colours

For softer pinks, mauves and blues, look at papery flowers such as oriental poppies, roses and peonies in cooler shades. The names may give clues: peony 'Mother of Pearl', for instance, or the roses 'Great Maiden's Blush' or 'New Dawn'. Irises come in stunning shades from dark *Iris chrysographes* to the pale lilacs of some Siberian or Reticulata varieties. From the many cool-coloured clematis, 'Etoile Violette', 'Elsa Späth' and 'Perle d'Azur' are among the best mauves, and purple-centred white *C. florida* 'Sieboldii' has stylish flowers. Canterbury bells (*Campanula medium*) and monkshood (*Aconitum*) also give strong mauves fading to white. Mix clear blues with darker purples and wine reds, and complement flower colour with silvery grey foliage. Or try subtly two-toned plants such as the pink-tinged forms of *Astrantia major* or the mauve and pink *Salvia sclarea* var. *turkestanica*.

wild new cottage garden

A mix of traditional border plants in bright blowsy colours, strong foliage interest and a few striking vegetables is the key to this look. Poppies and peonies will never be out of place; the dusky oriental poppy 'Patty's Plum' is particularly desirable – its colour is like pink silk dipped in weak tea. Thistle-like plants such as sea holly, *Eryngium alpinum*, with its filigree blue bracts, or magenta-headed *Cirsium rivulare* 'Atropurpureum' are fashionable, and go well with star-like astrantias, in pure white to pink-tinged and the crimson of 'Hadspen Blood' or 'Ruby Wedding'. Vegetables that add height or interesting leaves, like globe artichokes, purple-sprouting broccoli or runner beans on poles or teepees, are welcome among the flowers. Ornamental onions such as *Allium cristophii* and 'Purple Sensation' link vegetables and flowers with style.

Left The fashionable dusky pink of the oriental poppy, *Papaver orientale* 'Patty's Plum'.
Below *Phlomis amazonica* is another strong sculptural plant that is becoming more widely known. It looks good among Mediterranean plants and grasses, and because it can tolerate dry soils is a good gravel garden choice.

Right The deep crimson flowers and attractive leaves of *Rosa moyesii*. This species rose is a superb shrub rose that does well in light shade and is remarkable for the coronet of yellow stamens in the centre of each bloom. It has flagon-shaped, bright red hips in autumn.

Right The best cottage gardens are a mix of flowers and vegetables – this leek, left to go to seed, is just bursting into flower.

Below Love-in-a-mist or *Nigella* is no less beautiful for being so widespread. Its delicate whiskery blooms are as welcome in the border, where it self-seeds readily, as they are arranged in small posies of flowers about the house.

Left The beautiful deep blue flowers of *Anchusa azurea*. This short-lived perennial enjoys deep, well-drained soil.

Below Chives (*Allium schoenoprasum*) have attractive pink flowers as well as tasty leaves. They make a neat edging plant and look particularly good planted beneath roses.

Right Leeks gone to seed provide
height and drama in the border,
if not the intense colours of their
ornamental allium cousins. Decorative
seed-heads are a good way of adding
autumn and winter interest.

Left Giant hogweed (*Heracleum
mantegazzianum*) is stunning.
Growing to more than 3.6 m (12 ft)
tall, its architectural form looks
impressive at the back of a border or
on the fringes of woodland, but it is
poisonous, so it is not recommended
where children could brush against it.

Right The loose mop-head blooms of
Hydrangea arborescens form a beautiful
blowsy cloud up to 2.4 m (8 ft) tall and wide.
Frost-hardy and shade-loving, its snowy white
flowers are formed in late spring, emerging
from tight clusters of buds and then turning
green with age. Many of the other white
forms of hydrangea create a similar effect.

giants in the border

Spires of flowering plants punctuate a bed or border like splendid exclamation marks, even when springing up as singles or small groups near the front of a border. Must-have tall plants include foxgloves, especially the large-flowered white-spotted varieties and the delicate, bronze-flowered *Digitalis ferruginea*; delphiniums in every shade from deep purple to cobalt blue and softest lilac; white and deep purple monkshood (*Aconitum carmichaelii*); peachy foxtail lilies (*Eremurus*) and a host of lupins and salvias. The spherical heads of the larger alliums such as *A. giganteum* and delicate starry *A. cristophii* will vary the form. Tall plants with a semi-transparent habit, like spindly *Verbena bonariensis*, can be used to create a hazy 'screen' or mingle with ornamental grasses.

Left above Thalictrums, with their fuzzy candyfloss blooms, grow to 1.8 m (6 ft) or more and create strong splashes of colour in the border.
Left The Scotch thistle (*Onopordum acanthium*) has the famous light purple flowers shown on the Scottish national emblem. The plant grows to 3 m (10 ft) or more and has indented prickly leaves.

Left *Digitalis ferruginea*, sometimes called the rusty foxglove, has small golden brown flowers on sweeping spires that look fantastic in wild or woodland plantings. Long after the flowers have faded, the dried stems contribute a strong vertical element to the border. The seeds will disperse to crop up as new plants in unexpected places.

Left The cardoon (*Cynara cardunculus*) has sculptural flower heads on towering stems as well as scrolling silver leaves – all in all a dramatic addition to any border. The blanched stems, but not the heads, are also edible.

Below Moisture-loving *Gunnera manicata*, the giant rhubarb, has an almost prehistoric quality – its leaves open into huge umbrellas many feet across and the flowers resemble miniature Tamil temples.

architectural foliage Plants with strong foliage give a
garden style and identity – and evergreens, of course, are effective right through the winter. Ornamental grasses, among the most fashionable foliage plants for the new country garden, range from the bold silhouettes of giants like *Stipa gigantea* to the silky mauve seed-heads of *Miscanthus sinensis* and the pale fluffy plumes of the pennisetums. Their seed-heads provide stunning effects throughout summer and into autumn and winter, when the low light and an outline of frost show them to great advantage. Other good foliage plants include all the hostas, whose large, ridged leaves have a strong sculptural presence; silvery leaved plants such as senecios, santolinas and helichrysums (all of which do well in strong sun and by the sea), and the wonderful glaucous grey leaves of *Macleaya cordata*, a herbaceous perennial that can top 3.6 m (12 ft) in a summer.

Right Hostas are well known as stunning foliage plants – provided you can protect them from slugs, who love to feast on the splendid ridged leaves. There are hundreds of different hosta varieties, many offering variegation in the foliage.

Below One of the many decorative sea hollies, *Eryngium alpinum* has delicate filigree bracts around the central flower head.

Below The common mullein (*Verbascum*) shoots up a spire of yellow flowers from a rosette of woolly grey-green leaves. Its stately stature and long flowering season make it a desirable addition to the garden – unlike many of the other plants whose flowers form a spire, such as foxgloves and delphiniums, the flowers do not open from the bottom up, but a few at a time along the spike.

Right *Lobelia* 'Queen Victoria' has bright scarlet flowers above glamorous bronze foliage. It likes rich deep soil and associates well with dahlias and (as here) crocosmias.

Centre right *Potentilla* 'William Rollison' is a truly stunning plant, with splashes of orange at the edges of the bright red petals and attractive foliage. It flowers obligingly all summer.

Far right The unusual orange euphorbia, *E. griffithii* 'Fireglow' – once seen, always remembered for its flame-coloured bracts.

Above Bearded irises come in an extraordinarily wide range of colours – almost everything except for true red. The dusky purply-red of 'Hell's Fire' is as stunning as it is unusual. Like all bearded irises, it flowers in late spring and associates particularly well with roses; its sword-shaped grey-green foliage is also extremely attractive.

Above *Cerinthe major* 'Purpurascens' is rightly popular for its peacock-blue bracts and electric violet flowers. It is easy to grow and self-seeds readily around the garden.

Right The herbaceous clematis *Clematis integrifolia* has delicate spidery blooms. It can be grown up a support in the border.

unusual accent plants

There will always be plants in a bed or border that cry out to be noticed. Among these are the newly fashionable *Cerinthe major* 'Purpurascens', whose peacock-blue bracts and electric violet flowers are quite irresistible, and partner well with other bright colours. It is easy to grow from seed, and self-seeds readily. Bearded and other irises always cause a stir. Near-black velvety *Iris chrysographes* looks good against the feathery foliage of bronze fennel; the black and lime-green flowers of *Iris tuberosa* and the tawny ochre 'Marshlander' and 'Quechee' are heart-stopping. Turk's-head lilies with their delicately curled petals, bold-flowered clematis and roses like the deep claret 'Tuscany Superb' also draw the eye. Make sure you distribute these 'show-stoppers' throughout the garden, and that something else is waiting in the wings for when their glory fades.

Above Dahlias are always useful as accent plants – this one, 'Fascination', is a rich pink. 'Conway', 'Pink Pastelle', and 'Wootton Cupid' are other good pink dahlias.

Right Ornamental alliums such as *Allium* 'Purple Sensation' are, in fact, great clusters of tiny flowers that can be seen emerging as minute buds and then opening in the sun. They are attractive at all stages of their development, making wonderful dried spheres.

Far right The common buttercup – always an appealing and reassuring presence in wildflower meadows – though not usually as welcome in the middle of the lawn.

Below right The spotted orchid, *Dactylorhiza elata*, has flower spikes 30 cm (1 ft) high made up of smaller, delicately speckled blooms.

the tiniest details

Getting the details right is one of the crucial aspects of good gardening. Just as the eye needs bold concepts and strong lines to follow when it looks up to take in the whole scene, it also longs, butterfly-like, to settle on one perfect bloom or appreciate the texture of individual leaves and petals. The garden writer Mirabel Osler wittily divided garden visitors into 'crouchers and gapers': 'the former so set on plant spotting that they miss the larger picture, while the latter wander wide-eyed and miss all the details'. Plants that are structurally useful in a border but also offer interesting detail at close range include *Alchemilla mollis*, for its tiny lime-green flowers and habit of collecting dew drops in its fan-shaped leaves, and the many different types of euphorbia, whose fresh green bracts, sometimes with a contrasting deep maroon 'eye', are especially stunning in spring. Look for plants that are interesting at all stages of their unfolding – to watch an allium open over the space of a week or so is a wonder of nature, while roses with attractive hips, or other flowers with sculptural seed-heads, extend the usefulness of the plants long after their blooms have faded. Well positioned, even relatively humble plants such as the elderflower or buttercup can provide stunning effects, bringing some of the wildness of the wider landscape to the garden.

Left *Allium cristophii* have large balloon-like heads of starry purple flowers. They are one of the most beautiful of all the alliums, whether in full bloom or as a dried seed-head, but their shorter stems make them less easy to use in the border than some of their taller relatives.

Right The minaret-like heads of leeks gone to seed are a striking, somehow surreal presence in the garden.

Below The Shirley poppy (*Papaver rhoeas* Shirley Series) comes in unusual pastel shades from white and mother-of-pearl to pinks, reds and bicolours. Their delicate papery blooms are borne on fine hairy stems – horticultural beauty at its most ephemeral.

directory

NURSERIES WITH MAIL ORDER

APPLE COURT NURSERY
Hordle Lane
Hordle
Lymington
Hampshire SO41 OHU
(01590 642130)
Wonderful source for ornamental grasses, with a well-designed show garden where you can see all the varieties growing. Also stocks hostas, ferns and daylilies.

ARCHITECTURAL PLANTS
Cooks Farm
Nuthurst
Horsham
West Sussex RH13 6LH
(01403 891772)
Bold foliage plants are a speciality; helpful catalogue and knowledgeable staff; one of the best-designed nurseries around and well worth a visit.

CLAIRE AUSTIN HARDY PLANTS
Bowling Green Lane
Albrighton
Wolverhampton
West Midlands WV7 3HB
(01902 375481)
Great mail-order catalogue where all the plants are illustrated to help beginners choose what they want. Good for peonies in particular.

DAVID AUSTIN ROSES
Bowling Green Lane
Albrighton
Wolverhampton
West Midlands WV7 3HB
(01902 376376)
One of the best rose growers in the country, with an excellent mail-order track record. Well-illustrated catalogue ranges from ancient species to new arrivals.

THE BETH CHATTO GARDENS LTD
Elmstead Market
Colchester
Essex CO7 7DB
(01206 822007)
Plants specially selected for dry and gravel gardens, for shady areas and water gardens – all to be seen thriving in the wonderful display gardens.

COTSWOLD GARDEN FLOWERS
Sands Lane
Badsey
Evesham
Worcestershire WR11 5EZ
(01386 47337)
Specializes in easy and unusual perennials; the excellent catalogue gives plants a 'score' for appearance and easiness. Helpful staff.

DOWNDERRY NURSERY
Pillar Box Lane
Hadlow
Tonbridge
Kent TN11 9SW
(01732 810081)
The largest range of lavenders in Britain, set in a walled Victorian garden. Expert advice from the owner and a well-illustrated catalogue.

DE JAGER & SONS
The Nurseries
Staplehurst Road
Marden
Kent TN12 9BP
(01622 831345)
Top quality bulb specialists – well-illustrated catalogue with excellent selection of alliums, irises, tulips and unusual lilies.

OAKOVER NURSERIES
Maidstone Road
Hothfield
Ashford
Kent TN26 1AR
(01233 712424)
Hedging plants, from native hawthorn to neat box and yew for clipping, hornbeams and many trees. All grown on site and packed and sent well.

SARAH RAVEN'S CUTTING GARDEN
Perch Hill Farm
Brightling
Robertsbridge
East Sussex TN32 5HP
(01424 838181)
Bold and brilliant selection of flower seeds, selected for strong shapes and colours for cutting and arranging. Unusual vegetables also.

THE ROMANTIC GARDEN NURSERY
Swanington
Norwich
Norfolk NR9 5NW
(01603 261488)
All forms of topiary, well-trained into classic and unusual shapes. Not just box and yew – rosemary, lavender and citrus trees in all shapes and sizes.

DERRY WATKINS AT SPECIAL PLANTS
Greenways Lane
Cold Ashton
Chippenham
Wiltshire SN14 8LA
(01225 891686)
Hardy and tender perennials, with lots of conservatory and greenhouse rarities; modern garden around the house, open by appointment, shows plants in situ.

THE KITCHEN GARDEN

DEACONS NURSERY
Moor View
Godshill
Isle of Wight PO38 3HW
(01983 840750)
Late summer dessert apples, cider apples, quinces, walnuts, cherries, figs, plums and peaches, plus vines for the British climate.

GREEN GARDENER
41 Strumpshaw Road
Brundall
Norfolk NR13 5PG
(01603 715096)
Mail-order suppliers of biological pest controls, including nematodes to prey on slugs, vine weevils, aphids and other garden pests. Helpful and cheerful telephone advice service.

IDEN CROFT HERBS
Frittenden Road
Staplehurst
Kent TN12 ODH
(01580 891432)
Great collection of herbs, set in a wonderful romantic garden. Eleven types of basil, 13 rosemaries, 37 different mints – lots of unusual varieties.

THE ORGANIC GARDENING CATALOGUE
Riverdene Business Park
Molesey Road
Hersham
Surrey KT12 4RG
(01932 253666)
One of the best selections of vegetable seeds, including many organically grown varieties. Useful accessories for kitchen gardens.

SIMPSONS SEEDS
The Walled Garden Nursery
Horningsham
Warminster
Wiltshire BA12 7NQ
(01985 845004)
Famous for their tomatoes – seed for a large number of varieties and many sold as young plants. Also young 'plug' plants of courgettes, aubergines, peppers and cucumbers.

GARDEN ELEMENTS

CAPITAL GARDEN PRODUCTS
(01580 201092)
Topiary wire frames – flat-pack spirals and cones in various sizes.

TOM CLARK
18 Church Street
Martock
Somerset TA12 6JL
(01935 822111)
Stone carving and sculpture.

CLIFTON NURSERIES
5A Clifton Villas
London W9 2PH
(020 7289 6851)
Good stylish garden accessories, plus some one-off pieces and antiques.

CROWTHER OF SYON LODGE
Busch Corner
London Road
Isleworth TW7 5BH
(020 8560 7978)
Garden ornaments, from huge antique stone fountains to lead planters and smaller, figurative sculpture.

ANTHONY DE GREY TRELLISES
Broadhinton Yard
77A North Street
London SW4 OHQ
(020 7738 8866)
Architectural trellises made to order in a range of designs, plus arbour seats, gazebos, pergolas, pavilions, planters and decking.

DAVID HARBER SUNDIALS
The Sundial Workshop
Valley Farm
Bix
Henley-on-Thames
Oxfordshire RG9 6BW
(01491 576956)
Sundials in classic and contemporary designs – or commission your own.

HOMESTEAD TIMBER BUILDINGS
Wyndham House
Lupton Road
Wallingford
Oxfordshire OX10 9TD
(01491 838379)
A variety of classic sheds, summerhouses and garden offices, plus the opportunity to commission a building of your own design.

JARDINIQUE
Old Park Farm
Kings Hill
Beech
Alton
Hampshire GU34 4AW
(01420 560055)
Unusual garden antiques, handmade pots and more.

POTS AND PITHOI
The Barns
East Street
Turners Hill
West Sussex RH10 4QQ
(01342 714793)
Wonderful selection of handmade terracotta urns made by potters in Crete. Also a selection of antique pots and containers.

ROOM IN THE GARDEN
Oak Cottage
Furzen Lane
Ellens Green
Rudgwick
West Sussex RH12 3AR
(01403 823958)
Jan Howard's attractive 'rusted' iron plant supports and obelisks, chunky wooden furniture and gorgeous Gothic pavilions, complete with candelabra.

TRITON CASTING
Torbay Road Trading Estate
Torbay Road
Castle Cary
Somerset BA7 7DT
(01963 351653)
High quality reproduction stone casting.

FLOORS, WALLS AND FENCES

BRAMPTON WILLOWS
Upper Farm
Brampton
Beccles
Suffolk NR34 8EH
(01502 575891)
Woven willow bespoke fencing, constructed in situ.

DORSET RECLAMATION
Cow Drove
Bere Regis
Wareham
Dorset BH20 7JZ
(01929 472200)
Reclaimed flagstones, paving bricks and quarry tiles for creating your own paths and terraces that will look as if they have been in place for ever.

ENGLISH HURDLE
Curload
Stoke Street
Gregory
Taunton
Somerset TA3 6JD
(01823 690109)
Hurdle fence panels, plus materials for DIY willow structures and a good range of courses.

FOREST GARDEN
Stanford Court
Stanford Bridge
nr Worcester WR6 6SR
(01886 812451)
Fencing panels and wooden trellis.

SOIL AND COMPOST

FAIR FIELD TURF
Fairfield Court
Brookland
Romney Marsh
Kent TN29 9RX
(01797 344731)
Range of soils and turf delivered nationwide.

GLENFIELDS ORGANIC
Glenfield Farm
Haselbury
Crewkerne
Somerset TA18 7NZ
(01460 73251)
Peat-free soils and compost.

GREENFIX LTD
Harcourt Mews
Royal Crescent
Cheltenham
Gloucestershire GL50 3DA
(01242 700092)
Specialists in soil stabilization and erosion control.

OUTDOOR LIVING

THE CONRAN SHOP
Michelin House
81 Fulham Road
London SW3 6RD
(020 7589 7401)
Constantly changing stock of garden accessories, including lanterns, galvanized metal buckets, wooden plant labels, cricket chairs and hammocks.

DESIGNERS GUILD
267–71 Kings Road
London SW3 5EN
(020 7351 5775)
Brightly-coloured fabrics and table linen, simple but stylish bowls and crockery, wonderful cushions, striped and trimmed rugs. Mail order available.

GARDEN LIGHTING COMPANY
(01706 227525)
Garden lighting for entertaining and security purposes.

GAZE BURVILL
Newtonwood Workshop
Newton Vallance
Alton
Hants GU34 3EW
(01420 587467)
Well-made contemporary and traditional furniture.

JASON GRIFFITHS
Higher Tideford
Cornworthy
Totnes
Devon TQ9 7HL
(07971 921676)
Coppiced wood furniture in a range of styles, plus hurdle panels.

HABITAT
196 Tottenham Court Road
London W1T 7LG
(020 7631 3880)
Good for seasonal garden furniture including simple folding chairs and tables in strong colours that look good in modern and traditional style gardens.

CATH KIDSTON
8 Clarendon Cross
London W11 4AP
(020 7221 4248)
Great selection of old striped Welsh blankets in sugary colours, plus fabrics and accessories in gloriously retro designs. Mail order available.

garden designers whose work is featured in this book

De Brinkhof Garden & Nursery
Dorpsstraat 46
Hernen 6616AJ
Holland
t. +31 487 531 486
Nursery and garden open every Tuesday, Friday and Saturday from 10am to 5pm, from April until the end of September. A small nursery specializing in hardy perennials, old-fashioned and unusual varieties.
Pages: 4 *c*, 16 *r*, 20, 28, 42 *l*, 52 *l*, 52–53, 54 *l*, 58–59, 82–83, 86 *b*, 86–87, 96 *al*, 100 *l*, 104, 106 *b*, 120–121, 121 *l*

Bryan's Ground Garden Design
t. 01544 260001
Pages: 36 *r*, 38–39, 44 *r*, 92 *l*

Tania Compton
taniacompton@madasafish.com
Pages: 2–3, 10 *bl*, 17, 18, 19, 22–23, 30–31, 41 *a*, 44 *l*, 47 *a*, 56 *br*, 87 *r*, 100–101

Cooper/Taggart Designs
t. +1 323 256 3048
coopertaggart@earthlink.net
Pages: 50 *b*, 95 *r*

Huys de Dohm
Heerlen
The Netherlands
t. +31 455 710 470
Pages: 16 *b*, 38 *l*, 48 *b*, 61 *l*, 62 *l*, 63 *l*, 90 *l* & *br*, 91 *r*, 102 *l*, 103 *al*

Nancy Goslee Power & Associates
1660 Stanford Street
Santa Monica
CA 90404
USA
t. +1 310 264 0266
f. +1 310 264 0268
ngpa@flash.net
Pages: 93 *l*, 117 *r*

Isabelle C. Greene, F.A.S.L.A.
Isabelle Greene & Associates
Landscape Architects and Land Planners
2613 De la Vina Street
Santa Barbara
CA 93105
USA
t. +1 805 569 4045
icgreene@aol.com
Page: 45

Ivan Hicks
Garden and Landscape Designer, Land Artist
Hurdley Moor Farm
Middlemarsh
Sherborne
Dorset DTN 5QN
t./f. 01963 210886
Pages: 110 *a* & *bl*, 111

Judy Kameon
Elysian Landscapes
724 Academy Road
Los Angeles
CA 90012
USA
t. +1 323 226 9588
f. +1 323 226 1191
www.elysianlandscapes.com
Page: 49

Peter & Pam Lewis
Garden Design, Restoration & Management
Sticky Wicket
Buckland Newton
Dorchester
Dorset DT2 7BY
t./f. 01300 345476
Pages: 15, 25, 26–27, 29 *b*, 51, 61 *r*, 68 *a*, 78–79, 85 *l*, 107, 137 *al* & *r*, endpapers

Mill Cottage Plants
Henley Mill
Wookey
Somerset BA5 1AW
t. 01749 676966

Christina Oates
Secret Garden Designs
Fovant Hut
Fovant
Nr. Salisbury
Wiltshire SP3 5LN
t. 01722 714756
www.secretgardendesigns.co.uk
Garden designer Christina Oates specializes in imaginative and yet down-to-earth consultancy visits and concept plans.
Pages: 1, 5, 66 *l*, 70, 105, 118 *r*

Sarah Raven's Cutting Garden
Perch Hill Farm
Brightling
Robertsbridge
East Sussex TN32 5HP
t. 01424 838181
f. 01424 838571
info@thecuttinggarden.com
www.thecuttinggarden.com
Pages: 10 *a*, 12–13, 92 *br*, 106 *al*, 109 *l*

Jan Howard
Room in the Garden
Oak Cottage
Furzen Lane
Ellens Green
Rudgwick
West Sussex RH12 3AR
t./f. 01403 823958
Manufacturers of elegant designs in rusted iron. Garden design services by Jan Howard. Catalogue available.
Pages: 3 *r*, 42 *r*, 57, 96 *bl*, 112 *l* & *r*, 113 *l* & *r*

Marc Schoellen
Garden Historian & Amateur Garden Designer
35, route de Colmar-Berg
L-7525 Mersch
Grand-Duché
Luxembourg
t. +352 327 269
Pages: 30 *l*, 67 *r*, 88–89, 102–103, 103 *r*, 110 *r*, 116 *al*, 119 *l*

Tom Stuart-Smith
3rd Floor
Kirkman House
12–14 Whitfield Street
London W1P 5RD
Pages: 34–35, 36 *bl*, 74–75, 76 *a*, 112 *ac*

Derry Watkins
Special Plants
Greenways Lane
Cold Ashton
Chippenham
Wiltshire SN14 8LA
t. 01225 891686
specialplants@bigfoot.com
www.specialplants.net
Opening hours 10.30am to 4.30pm March to September, other times by arrangement; mail order September to March only; please send five second class stamps for catalogue.
Pages: 16 *a*, 24, 40–41, 60 *l*, 93 *r*, 97, 108 *l*, 109 *r*, 116 *b*

picture credits

Key: *a*=above, *b*=below, *l*=left, *r*=right, *c*=centre

All photographs by Melanie Eclare.
1 Fovant Hut Garden near Salisbury in Wiltshire was created by garden designer Christina Oates together with her husband Nigel and is open to the public;
2–3 Peter and Sandra Aitken-Quack's garden at Ham Cross Farm near Tisbury, designed by Tania Compton; 3 *r* Jan Howard's garden in Sussex; 4 *c* The garden and nursery De Brinkhof of Riet Brinkhof and Joop Van Den Berk; 4 *b* Connie Haydon's garden in Dorset; 5 Fovant Hut Garden near Salisbury in Wiltshire was created by garden designer Christina Oates together with her husband Nigel and is open to the public; 8–9 Niall Manning and Alastair Morton's garden, Dunard, Fintry, Scotland; 10 *a* Sarah Raven's Cutting Garden in Brightling, designed by Sarah Raven; 10 *bl* Peter and Sandra Aitken-Quack's garden at Ham Cross Farm near Tisbury, designed by Tania Compton; 10–11 Daphne Shackleton's garden in

Co. Cavan, Ireland; 12–13 Sarah Raven's Cutting Garden in Brightling, designed by Sarah Raven; 14 *a* Connie Haydon's garden in Dorset; 14 *b* Jim Reynolds' garden 'Butterstream', Co. Meath, Ireland; 15 Sticky Wicket wildlife garden near Dorchester, designed and created by Peter and Pam Lewis; 16 *a* Derry Watkins' garden in Wiltshire designed by Derry Watkins and her husband, the architect Peter Clegg; 16 *b* Ineke Greve, gardens of 'Huys de Dohm' Heerlen, The Netherlands; 16 *r* The garden and nursery De Brinkhof of Riet Brinkhof and Joop Van Den Berk; 17, 18 & 19 Peter and Sandra Aitken-Quack's garden at Ham Cross Farm near Tisbury, designed by Tania Compton; 20 The garden and nursery De Brinkhof of Riet Brinkhof and Joop Van Den Berk; 20–21 & 21 *r* Connie Haydon's garden in Dorset; 22 *l* Daphne Shackleton's garden in Co. Cavan, Ireland; 22–23 Peter and Sandra Aitken-Quack's garden at Ham Cross Farm near Tisbury, designed by Tania Compton; 24 Derry Watkins' garden in Wiltshire designed by Derry Watkins and her husband, the architect Peter Clegg; 25 & 26–27 Sticky Wicket wildlife garden near Dorchester, designed and created by

Peter and Pam Lewis; 28 The garden and nursery De Brinkhof of Riet Brinkhof and Joop Van Den Berk; 29 *a* Jim Reynolds' garden 'Butterstream', Co. Meath, Ireland; 29 *b* Sticky Wicket wildlife garden near Dorchester, designed and created by Peter and Pam Lewis; 30 *l* Marc Schoellen's garden in Luxembourg called 'La Bergerie'; 30–31 Peter and Sandra Aitken-Quack's garden at Ham Cross Farm near Tisbury, designed by Tania Compton; 32 *b* & 32–33 Mr. and Mrs. James Hepworth's garden in Herefordshire; 33 *r* Jim Reynolds' garden 'Butterstream', Co. Meath, Ireland; 34–35 & 36 *bl* Tom Stuart-Smith's garden in Hertfordshire; 36 *r* Bryan's Ground, David Wheeler and Simon Dorrell's garden in Herefordshire; 37 Niall Manning and Alastair Morton's garden, Dunard, Fintry, Scotland; 38 *l* Ineke Greve, gardens of 'Huys de Dohm' Heerlen, The Netherlands; 38–39 Bryan's Ground, David Wheeler and Simon Dorrell's garden in Herefordshire; 40–41 Derry Watkins' garden in Wiltshire designed by Derry Watkins and her husband, the architect Peter Clegg; 41 *a* Peter and Sandra Aitken-Quack's garden at Ham Cross Farm near Tisbury, designed by Tania Compton; 42 *l* The garden and nursery of De Brinkhof of Riet Brinkhof and Joop Van Den Berk; 42 *r* Jan Howard's garden in Sussex; 43 Jim Reynolds' garden 'Butterstream', Co. Meath, Ireland; 44 *l* Peter and Sandra Aitken-Quack's garden at Ham Cross Farm near Tisbury, designed by Tania Compton; 44 *r* Bryan's Ground, David Wheeler and Simon Dorrell's garden in Herefordshire; 45 Carol Valentine's garden in California, designed by Isabelle Greene, F.A.S.L.A. a California Landscape Architect; 46–47 Niall Manning and Alastair Morton's garden, Dunard, Fintry, Scotland; 47 *a* Peter and Sandra Aitken-Quack's garden at Ham Cross Farm near Tisbury, designed by Tania Compton; 48 *a* Jim Reynolds' garden 'Butterstream', Co. Meath, Ireland; 48 *b* Ineke Greve, gardens of 'Huys de Dohm' Heerlen, The Netherlands; 49 Garden in Los Angeles designed by Judy Kameon – Elysian Landscapes; 50 *a* The Farrell family, Woodnewton; 50 *b* Laura Cooper and Nick Taggart's Los Angeles garden, designed by Cooper/Taggart Designs; 51 Sticky Wicket wildlife garden near Dorchester, designed and created by Peter and Pam Lewis; 52 *l* & 52–53 The garden and nursery De Brinkhof of Riet Brinkhof and Joop Van Den Berk; 52 *b* Mr. and Mrs. James Hepworth's garden in Herefordshire; 53 *r* The Farrell family, Woodnewton; 54 *l* The garden and nursery of De Brinkhof of Riet Brinkhof and Joop Van Den Berk; 54 *br* The Farrell family, Woodnewton; 54 *a* & 55 Mr. and Mrs. James Hepworth's garden in Herefordshire; 56 *a* & *bl* Jim Reynold's garden 'Butterstream', Co. Meath, Ireland; 56 *br* Peter and Sandra Aitken-Quack's garden at Ham Cross Farm near Tisbury, designed by Tania Compton; 57 Jan Howard's garden in Sussex; 58–59 The garden and nursery De Brinkhof of Riet Brinkhof and Joop Van Den Berk; 60 *l* Derry Watkins' garden in Wiltshire designed by Derry Watkins and her husband, the architect Peter Clegg; 60 *r* Mr. and Mrs. James Hepworth's garden in Herefordshire; 61 *l* Ineke Greve, gardens of 'Huys de Dohm' Heerlen, The Netherlands; 61 *r* Sticky Wicket wildlife garden near Dorchester, designed and created by Peter and Pam Lewis; 62 *l* & 63 *l* Ineke Greve, gardens of 'Huys de Dohm' Heerlen, The Netherlands; 62 *r* Connie Haydon's garden in Dorset; 64–65 Cranborne Manor, Dorset; 66 *l* Fovant Hut Garden near Salisbury in Wiltshire was created by garden designer Christina Oates together with her husband Nigel and is open to the public; 67 *r* Marc Schoellen's garden in Luxembourg called 'La Bergerie'; 68 *a* Sticky Wicket wildlife garden near Dorchester, designed and created by Peter and Pam Lewis; 68–69 Niall Manning and Alastair Morton's garden, Dunard, Fintry, Scotland; 70 Fovant Hut Garden near Salisbury in Wiltshire was created by garden designer Christina Oates together with her husband Nigel and is open to the public; 74–75 & 76 *a* Tom Stuart-Smith's garden in Hertfordshire; 76–77 Connie Haydon's garden in Dorset; 78–79 Sticky Wicket wildlife garden near Dorchester, designed and created by Peter and Pam Lewis; 80–81 Connie Haydon's garden in Dorset; 82–83 The garden and

nursery De Brinkhof of Riet Brinkhof and Joop Van Den Berk; 84 *a* & *b* Niall Manning and Alastair Morton's garden, Dunard, Fintry, Scotland; 85 *l* Sticky Wicket wildlife garden near Dorchester, designed and created by Peter and Pam Lewis; 85 *r* Jim Reynolds' garden 'Butterstream', Co. Meath, Ireland; 86–87 & 86 *b* The garden and nursery De Brinkhof of Riet Brinkhof and Joop Van Den Berk; 87 *r* Peter and Sandra Aitken-Quack's garden at Ham Cross Farm near Tisbury, designed by Tania Compton; 88–89 Marc Schoellen's garden in Luxembourg called 'La Bergerie'; 90 *l* & *br* & 91 *r* Ineke Greve, gardens of 'Huys de Dohm' Heerlen, The Netherlands; 90–91 Jim Reynolds' garden 'Butterstream', Co. Meath, Ireland; 92 *l* Bryan's Ground, David Wheeler and Simon Dorrell's garden in Herefordshire; 92 *a* Niall Manning and Alastair Morton's garden, Dunard, Fintry, Scotland; 92 *br* Sarah Raven's Cutting Garden in Brightling, designed by Sarah Raven; 93 *l* Nancy Goslee Power, garden designer, Los Angeles; 93 *r* Derry Watkins' garden in Wiltshire designed by Derry Watkins and her husband, the architect Peter Clegg; 94 *b* Connie Haydon's garden in Dorset; 94 *a* Mr. and Mrs. James Hepworth's garden in Herefordshire; 95 *l* Jim Reynolds' garden 'Butterstream', Co. Meath, Ireland; 95 *r* Laura Cooper and Nick Taggart's Los Angeles garden, designed by Cooper/Taggart Designs; 96 *al* The garden and nursery De Brinkhof of Riet Brinkhof and Joop Van Den Berk; 96 *bl* Jan Howard's garden in Sussex; 96 *r* Jim Reynolds' garden 'Butterstream', Co. Meath, Ireland; 97 Derry Watkins' garden in Wiltshire designed by Derry Watkins and her husband, the architect Peter Clegg; 98–99 Connie Haydon's garden in Dorset; 100 *l* The garden and nursery De Brinkhof of Riet Brinkhof and Joop Van Den Berk; 100–101 Peter and Sandra Aitken-Quack's garden at Ham Cross Farm near Tisbury, designed by Tania Compton; 102 *l* & 103 *al* Ineke Greve, gardens of 'Huys de Dohm' Heerlen, The Netherlands; 102–103 & 103 *r* Marc Schoellen's garden in Luxembourg called 'La Bergerie'; 104 The garden and nursery De Brinkhof of Riet Brinkhof and Joop Van Den Berk; 105 Fovant Hut Garden near Salisbury in Wiltshire was created by garden designer Christina Oates together with her husband Nigel and is open to the public; 106 *al* Sarah Raven's Cutting Garden in Brightling, designed by Sarah Raven; 106 *ar* Jim Reynolds' garden 'Butterstream', Co. Meath, Ireland; 106 *b* The garden and nursery De Brinkhof of Riet Brinkhof and Joop Van Den Berk; 107 Sticky Wicket wildlife garden near Dorchester, designed and created by Peter and Pam Lewis; 108 *l* Derry Watkins' garden in Wiltshire designed by Derry Watkins and her husband, the architect Peter Clegg; 108 *r* Jim Reynolds' garden 'Butterstream', Co. Meath, Ireland; 109 *l* Sarah Raven's Cutting Garden in Brightling, designed by Sarah Raven; 109 *r* Derry Watkins' garden in Wiltshire designed by Derry Watkins and her husband, the architect Peter Clegg; 110 *a* & *bl* & 111 Mart Barlow's garden designed by Ivan Hicks; 110 *r* Marc Schoellen's garden in Luxembourg called 'La Bergerie'; 112 *l* & *r* & 113 *l* & *r* Jan Howard's garden in Sussex; 112 *ac* Tom Stuart-Smith's garden in Hertfordshire; 112 *br* Mr. and Mrs. James Hepworth's garden in Herefordshire; 114–115 Niall Manning and Alastair Morton's garden, Dunard, Fintry, Scotland; 115 *r* Jim Reynolds' garden 'Butterstream', Co. Meath, Ireland; 116 *al* Marc Schoellen's garden in Luxembourg called 'La Bergerie'; 116 *bl* Derry Watkins' garden in Wiltshire designed by Derry Watkins and her husband, the architect Peter Clegg; 116–117 The Farrell family, Woodnewton; 117 *r* Nancy Goslee Power, garden designer, Los Angeles; 118 *r* Fovant Hut Garden near Salisbury in Wiltshire was created by garden designer Christina Oates together with her husband Nigel and is open to the public; 119 *l* Marc Schoellen's garden in Luxembourg called 'La Bergerie'; 120–121 & 121 *l* The garden and nursery De Brinkhof of Riet Brinkhof and Joop Van Den Berk; 137 *al* & *r* Sticky Wicket wildlife garden near Dorchester, designed and created by Peter and Pam Lewis; **Endpapers** Sticky Wicket wildlife garden near Dorchester, designed and created by Peter and Pam Lewis.

index

Figures in *italics* refer to captions.

A

acers, Japanese, *48*
achilleas (yarrow), *125*
   A. 'Fanal', *125*
   A. millefolium 'Fire King', 124
   A. ptarmica 'The Pearl', *14*
Aconitum (monkshood), *16*, 22, 127
   A. carmichaelii, 131
agapanthus, *28*, *112*
Akebia quinata, 104
Alchemilla mollis (lady's mantle), 21, *94*, *121*, 136
allées, 40, *85*, *88*, *90*, 100, *119*
alliums, *12*, *25*, *28*, 71
   A. cristophii, *27*, *28*, 128, 131, *137*
   A. giganteum, *10*, 131
   A. 'Purple Sensation', *71*, 128, *136*
   A. schoenoprasum (chives), *129*
   drumstick, 29
almond trees, *44*
Anaphalis, 28
   A. triplinervis (pearly everlasting), 28
Anchusa azurea, *129*
Anthemis arvensis (corn chamomile), *66*
Anthriscus sylvestris (cow parsley), *64*, *66*, *71*
aphids, 63, 66
apple trees, 61, *108*
Aquilegia 'Magpie', 21, *38*, *122*
arbours, 100
arches, *28*, *48*, *48*, *62*, *63*, *85*, *92*, *94*, *94*, *104*, 106, *107*
Arctotis hirsuta (African daisy), *124*
art in the garden, 104, 108
Artemisia, 110
artichokes
   globe, *63*, 128
   Roman, *38*
asters, 28
astrantias, *14*, 128
   A. major, *126*, 127
   A. major 'Hadspen Blood', *16*, 18, 128
   A. major 'Ruby Wedding', 128
awnings, 61

B

bamboo, 54, *63*, 93
barbecues, 50, 56
bay (Laurus nobilis), 35, *35*, 38, *42*, *62*, 103, *111*
beanpoles, 62
beans, 60, *63*
beech, 30, 43, *85*, *91*, 94, 115
Bellis perennis (daisy), *66*
benches, *43*, *97*, *100*, *102*
berries, 76
birds, 63, 64, 66, 68, 71, 74, 76, *76*, 121
blackfly, 63
bleeding heart (Dicentra spectabilis 'Alba'), *22*
bluebells, 17
bowers, 53–4, 61, *104*
box (Buxus), 30, *30*, *33*, 35, *36*, 38, *38*, *39*, *41*, *43*, *44*, *47*, *90*, *94*, *94*, *102*, 103
brick, 38–9, 88, *91*, *94*
bridges, *106*, 117
broad beans, 60
broccoli, purple-sprouting, 128
brooks, 115
buddleias, 76
   B. alternifolia, *25*
bulbs, spring, 17, 29, *64*
bulrushes, *117*
buttercups, *66*, 136, *136*
butterflies, 64, 68, 74, 76, *78*
Buxus see box

C

cabbages (brassicas), *63*
cacti, 50
cairns, *108*
Calamagrostis x acutiflora 'Stricta', 25
Calamagrostis brachytricha, 76
campanulas (C. lactiflora), *28*, *110*
   C. medium (Canterbury bells), 127
Canna x generalis (canna lily), 18
Canterbury bells (Campanula medium), 127
Cardamine pratensis (lady's smock), 71
cardoons (Cynara cardunculus), *12*, *35*, *132*
carexes, 25
carrots, *63*
castor oil plant (Ricinus communis 'Carmencita'), 124
catmint (Nepeta), *39*, 43, *47*

Cephalaria gigantea (giant scabious), *21*, *22*, *28*
Centranthus ruber 'Albus' (white valerian), *18*
Cercis siliquastrum (Judas tree), *71*
Cerinthe major 'Purpurascens', *112*, *134*, 135
Chaerophyllum hirsutum 'Roseum', *123*
chairs, 56, *56*, *59*, 61, *96*, *117*
chamomile, *27*, 39
   corn (Anthemis arvensis), *66*
Chatto, Beth, 14
chickens, 61
chicory, *63*
children, 53–4, 121
chives (Allium schoenoprasum), *129*
Cirsium rivulare 'Atropurpureum', *128*
clary sage (Salvia sclarea var. turkestanica), *18*, *35*, *126*, 127
clematis, 7, 22, *36*, 94, *104*
   C. 'Elsa Späth', 127
   C. 'Etoile Violette', 127
   C. florida 'Sieboldii', 127
   C. integrifolia, *134*
   C. 'Perle d'Azur', 127
   C. 'Tuscany Superb', 135
cloches, *63*
colonnades, *48*
colour, 18, 21, 124–7
convolvulus, *111*
   C. cneorum, 21
copper beech (Fagus sylvatica f. purpurea), 22, *85*
corn cockle, 72
cornflowers, 72
Cosmos, 38
courtyard gardens, *10*, *17*, *30*, *41*, *42*, *87*, *117*
cow parsley (Anthriscus sylvestris), *64*, *66*, *71*
crab apples (Malus), 76
Crambe cordifolia, *18*, *111*
Crataegus monogyna (hawthorn), 38, 43, 76, 94
creeping jenny (Lysimachia nummularia), 71
crocosmias, *11*, *41*, *134*
   C. 'Lucifer', *12*, 18
crocuses, *43*
currants, 63, 103
Cynara cardunculus (cardoon), *12*, *35*, *132*

D

Dactylorhiza elata (spotted orchid), *136*
daffodils, 63
dahlias, 18, *134*
   D. 'Bishop of Llandaff', 18, 124, *124*
   D. 'Conway', 135
   D. 'Fascination', 135
   D. 'Pink Pastelle', *135*
   D. 'Wootton Cupid', 135
daisies, *43*
   African (Arctotis hirsuta), 124
   common (Bellis perennis), 66
   Michaelmas, *11*
   ox-eye, moon (Leucanthemum vulgare), *66*, 72
damp gardens, 14
daylilies, 18, 124
   see also Hemerocallis
decking, 7, *115*, *119*
deer, 64
delphiniums, 11, *14*, *21*, 22, *121*, 131, *133*
   D. 'Alice Artindale', *98*
deschampsias, 25
designing the garden, 82–95
dianthus, alpine, *112*
Dicentra spectabilis 'Alba' (bleeding heart), *22*
Digitalis see foxgloves
dividing space, 88–93
dragonflies, 7, 121
driftwood, 39
dry stone walling, *41*, 91, *92*
ducks, 66

E

eating areas, 56, 61
echeverias, *94*
Echinacea, 28, *122*
   E. purpurea Elton Hybrids, *122*
elder, 63
elderflower, 136
endives, *63*
Epilobium angustifolium (rose bay willowherb), 28
Eremurus (foxtail lily), 22, *41*, 131
Erigeron karvinskianus, *94*
eryngiums (sea hollies), *14*, *68*
   E. alpinum, 128, *133*
   E. giganteum (Miss Willmott's ghost), *10*, 22
eschscholzias, *41*
   E. californica (California poppy), *124*, *125*

Eucomis bicolor (pineapple lily), *112*
Eupatorium purpureum (Joe Pye weed), *14*
euphorbias, *12*, *14*, 21, 136
   E. griffithii, *44*
   E. griffithii 'Fireglow', *134*
evening primrose, *94*
evergreens, 43, *102*, 132

F

Fagus sylvatica f. purpurea (copper beech), 22, *85*
fairy lights, 61
family gardens, 50–63
fences, 62, 64, *82*, *83*, *86*, 87, 88, *91*, *92*, 93, 104
fennel, *39*
ferns, 17
   asparagus, *48*
fig trees, 50
Finlay, Ian Hamilton, 44
flax, New Zealand (Phormium tenax 'Purpureum'), *25*
flint, 88, *108*
Foerster, Karl, 25
follies, 53, *53*
foot mazes, 43
formal gardens, 25, 30–49
fountains, *48*, *97*, 115, *116*
foxgloves (Digitalis), 22, *22*, *27*, *46*, *47*, 131, *133*
   D. purpurea 'Pam's Choice', *46*
   rusty (D. ferruginea), 131, *131*
fritillaries, 63
frogs, 66, *117*, 121
fruit trees, 63, *71*
fruits
   organic, 61
   soft, 63

G

garden features, 96–113
gazanias, 124
gazebos, *97*, 100
geraniums, *110*
   cranesbill, *27*
   G. 'Johnson's Blue', *28*
   G. phaeum, *25*
   hardy, 21–2
goats, *86*
Goldsworthy, Andy, 108, *110*
gooseberries, 103
grape hyacinths, 63
grapevines, 35, 36, *44*, *104*, *108*

grasses, 18, 25, *25*, *27*, 28, 29, 35, 43, *47*, *66*, *68*, 72, 74, *74*, 76
  cloud, *27*
  fountain, 22
  ornamental, 7, 11, 22, 30, *30*, 32, 38, *38*, *50*, *76*, *122*, 131, 132
  see also Stipa
gravel, 36, 38, *43*, 113
  gardens, 14, 17
Great Dixter, East Sussex, 18
Greene, Isabelle, 14
Gunnera manicata (giant rhubarb), *119*, *132*

H
hammocks, *56*, *100*
hawthorns (*Crataegus monogyna*), 38, 43, 76, 94
hazel, 35, 63, *110*
hedgehogs, 66
hedges, 11, 25, 30, *33*, 35, *35*, *36*, 38, *38*, *39*, 40, *41*, 43, *43*, 44, *44*, *47*, 48, *61*, 62, 63, 64, 76, 85, *86*, 87, *87*, 88, *88*, *90*, 91, 94, *94*, *102*, *108*, *115*, *119*
  topiary, *30*, 44
heleniums, 18
Helichrysum, 110, *112*, 132
hellebores
  Corsican (*Helleborus argutifolius*), *123*
  Helleborus foetidus, 21
Hemerocallis 'Aztec', 124
Hemerocallis 'Little Grapette', 18
Heracleum mantegazzianum (giant hogweed), 130
herbaceous borders, 21, 29
herbaceous plants, *32*
herbs, 17, *61*, 93
  herb gardens, 32, *60*, 87
  herb wheels, 43
Hesperis matronalis var. *albiflora* (white rocket), *17*
Hicks, David, 118
Hicks, Ivan, 108, *108*
hideaways, 53, *53*, 54
hogweeds, giant (*Heracleum mantegazzianum*), 130
holly, 94, 103
hollyhocks, 11
honeysuckles, 94, *104*
hops, 21
hornbeams, *85*

horse chestnuts, *64*
hostas, 132, *133*
houseleeks, 39
Humulus lupulus 'Aureus', 21
hurdles, *92*, 93
Hydrangea arborescens, 130

I
insects, 63, *76*, 71, *78*, 121
Inula hookeri, *11*
irises, 7, *48*
  bearded, *134*, 135
  flag, 71, *117*, *119*
  I. 'Black Knight', 18
  I. chrysographes, 127, 135
  I. ensata, *122*
  I. 'Hell's Fire', *134*
  I. 'Marshlander', 135
  I. 'Quechee', 135
  I. sibirica, 44
  I. tuberosa, 135
ivy, 94

J
Joe Pye weed (*Eupatorium purpureum*), 14
Judas trees (*Cercis siliquastrum*), *71*
junipers, 36, *41*, *47*

K
kingcups, *117*
kitchen gardens, *42*, *50*, 61–2
Knautia macedonica, 18, *28*

L
lady's mantle (*Alchemilla mollis*), 21, *94*, *121*, 136
lady's smock (*Cardamine pratensis*), 71
Lathyrus sativus (sweet pea), 11, *16*, *62*, *106*, 111
Laurus nobilis (bay), 35, *35*, 38, *42*, *62*, 103, *111*
lavender, 21, 22, *47*, *92*, 93
lawns, *41*, 59, 66, 71, 72, *76*, 86, 87, *87*
  chamomile, *27*
  wildflower, 118
leeks, *129*, *130*, *137*
lettuces, *63*
Leucanthemum vulgare (moon daisy, ox-eye daisy), *66*, 72
lilies, *12*
  arum (*Zantedeschia aethiopica*), *119*

canna (*Canna* x *generalis*), 18
daylilies, 18, 124
foxtail (*Eremurus*), 22, *41*, 131
Lilium 'Fire King', 124
  pineapple (*Eucomis bicolor*), *112*
  regale, 39
  turk's-head, *12*, 135
  water, *115*, *121*
limes, 38, *85*, 100
limestone, 7, 38
Limnanthes douglasii (poached egg plant), 62–3
Linaria purpurea (toadflax), *72*
Lloyd, Christopher, 18
Lobelia 'Queen Victoria', *134*
London pride (*Saxifraga* x *urbium*), 17
Long, Richard, 108
loosestrife, purple (*Lythrum salicaria*), 14, 28
love-in-a-mist (*Nigella*), 11, *129*
lupins, 28, *41*, 131
Lychnis chalcedonica, 44
Lychnis coronaria 'Alba', 35
Lysimachia nummularia (creeping jenny), 71
Lythrum salicaria (purple loosestrife), 14, 28

M
Macleaya cordata (plume poppy), *74*, 132
mallows, 124
Malus (crab apple), 76
malvas, *111*
Meconopsis betonicifolia (Himalayan poppy), *126*
Meconopsis cambrica (Welsh poppy), *121*
mill ponds, 115, 117
mint, 43
mirrors, 48, *108*
Miscanthus sinensis, 28, 132
Miss Willmott's ghost (*Eryngium giganteum*), *10*, 22
mock orange (*Philadelphus*), 18, 68
monardas, 14, *71*, 76
monkshood (*Aconitum*), *16*, 22, 127, 131
Moon Gardens, 21
mosaics, 39
mulberry trees, *30*
mulleins (*Verbascum*), 35, *133*

N
narcissus, *43*
nasturtiums, 63, *111*
  N. 'Empress of India', 124
  N. 'Red Wonder', 124
nematodes, 66
Nepeta (catmint), *39*, 43, *47*
new perennial style, 22, 25
Nigella (love-in-a-mist), 11, *129*

O
oak, 94
obelisks, 22, *33*, 35, *36*, 46
Oehme, Wolfgang, 25
onions, ornamental, 128
  see also alliums
onoopordums, *12*
  O. acanthium (Scotch thistle), *131*
Ophiopogon planiscapus 'Nigrescens', 18
orchards, 44, *61*, 71
orchids, spotted (*Dactylorhiza elata*), *136*
oregano, *27*
organic growing, 7, 61–3, 66
Origanum, 28
  O. 'Kent Beauty', *41*
Osler, Mirabel, 136
Oudolf, Piet, 25, 28
outside rooms, 35–6

P
Paeonia lactiflora, *126*
Paeonia 'Mother of Pearl', 127
Panicum virgatum, 76
pansies, 21
Papaver see poppies
parterres, 35, 38, 48
paths, *27*, 30, *30*, *33*, 36, 40, *43*, *47*, 48, 62, *68*, 83, *85*, *86*, 88, *90*, 94, *119*
pavilions, 44
pearly everlastings (*Anaphalis triplinervis*), 28
pelargoniums, *112*
pennisetums, 132
  P. alopecuroides, *78*
  P. orientale, 25
peonies, *126*, 127
perennials, 22, 25, *32*, *36*
perfect plants, 122–37
pergolas, 35, 36, *90*
Permaculture, 66
Perovskia 'Blue Spire' (Russian sage), 21

Persicaria amplexicaulis, 14, *76*
pests, 62–3, 66, 68
Philadelphus (mock orange), *18*, 68
phlox, 14
phormiums, *41*
  P. tenax, *47*, *112*
  P. tenax 'Purpureum' (New Zealand flax), 25
physic gardens, 32
picket gates, *82*
plant containers, 110–13
plant groupings, 21–9
plant supports, 97, 104, *110*, *111*
planters, *43*, 93, *112*
poached egg plant (*Limnanthes douglasii*), 62–3
ponds, 7, *39*, 54, 68, 71, 115, 117, *119*, *121*
pools, 43, 48, *97*, *115*, *116*, 117, *117*, 118, 121
poppies, 44, 72, *74*, 128
  California (*Eschscholzia californica*), 124, *125*
  Himalayan (*Meconopsis betonicifolia*), *126*
  opium (*Papaver somniferum*), *126*
  oriental (*Papaver orientale*), 124, 127
  Papaver orientale Goliath Group, *10*
  Papaver orientale 'Patty's Plum', *16*, 128, *128*
  Papaver rhoeas, 66
  Papaver spicatum, *41*
  plume (*Macleaya cordata*), 74
  Shirley (*Papaver rhoeas* Shirley Series), *137*
  Welsh (*Meconopsis cambrica*), *121*
pot marigolds, 62–3
potagers, 7, 61, *61*
Potentilla 'William Rollison', *134*
pots, terracotta, *113*
primulas, candelabra (*Primula beesiana*), *121*
privet, 35

R
rabbits, 64
raised beds, *60*, 62
raspberries, 63
red hot pokers, 18
rhubarb, giant (*Gunnera manicata*), *119*, *132*

Ricinus communis 'Carmencita' (castor oil plant), 124
rills, 40, 48, 115
rock plants, *41*
rocket, white (*Hesperis matronalis* var. *albiflora*), *17*
Rosa see roses
rose bay willowherb (*Epilobium angustifolium*), *28*
roses, 7, 18, 36, *39*, *42*, *44*, 61, *106*, 127
climbing, *17*, *20*, *22*, *28*, 35, *36*, *41*, *100*, *104*
moss rose 'William Lobb', *72*
old, 44
rambling, *17*, *28*, 68
Rosa 'Cramoisi Supérieur', *125*
Rosa 'Ena Harkness', *125*
Rosa 'Great Maiden's Blush', 127
Rosa 'Iceberg', *17*
Rosa 'Lilli Marlene', *10*, 124, *125*
Rosa moyesii 'Geranium', *125*
Rosa 'New Dawn', 127
Rosa 'Paul's Himalayan Musk', *20*
Rosa rugosa, *28*, *86*, 94
Rosa 'Souvenir du Docteur Jamain', *125*
Rosa 'Tuscany Superb', *125*
rose gardens, *36*, 43, 87
training, *42*, *46*, 48
rowans (*Sorbus aucuparia*), 76
rudbeckias, 18, 28
runner beans, *60*, 128

S
Sackville-West, Vita, 21
sacred groves, 44
sages, 21
Russian (*Perovskia* 'Blue Spire'), 21
Salix caprea 'Kilmarnock' (Kilmarnock willow), 103
Salpiglossis 'Chocolate Pot', 124
salvias, 131
S. sclarea var. *turkestanica* (clary sage), *18*, *35*, *126*, 127
sandpits, 54, 121
Santolina, 21, 110, 132
Saxifraga x *urbium* (London pride), *17*
scabious, *28*
giant (*Cephalaria gigantea*), 21, *22*, *28*
sculpture, 97, 100, 104, 108, 118
sea hollies *see* eryngiums
seashells, *39*, 113
seating, *46*, *96*, 97, *97*, *99*, 100
see also chairs
Sedum, *28*, *110*
sempervivums (houseleeks), *39*
senecios, 132
Sidalcea malviflora, *11*, *22*
silver birch, 44
silver-leaved plants, 17, 21, *27*, 110, *112*, 127, 132
Sissinghurst, 21
slate, 38, 88

slugs, 62, 66, 68
snails, 62, 66
snowdrops, 44
soil-testing kits, 17
Sorbus aucuparia (rowan), 76
Stachys byzantina, 18
stepping stones, 117
steps, 48, *92*, 94
Stipa arundinacea (pheasant's tail grass), 25
Stipa calamagrostis, 28
Stipa gigantea (giant feather grass), *17*, *18*, 25, *25*, *33*, 132
Stipa tenuissima (feather grass), *14*, 25, *25*, *48*
strawberries, 93, *112*
streams, 17, *106*, 115
summerhouses, *36*, *50*, *53*, *61*, 84, 97, 100, *100*, 121
sundials, 100
sweet peas (*Lathyrus sativus*), 11, *16*, 62, *106*, *111*
swimming pools, 87
swings, 7, 53, 54, *54*, *86*

T
tables, *50*, 56, *56*, *59*, 61, *113*
Taxus see yew
terraces, 35, 40, 44, 87, 91
thalictrums, 124, *131*
T. delavayi, 22
thistles, Scotch (*Onopordum acanthium*), *131*

thyme, *27*, 39
tiles, 38–9, *117*
toadflax (*Linaria purpurea*), 72
toads, 66, 68, *117*, 121
topiary, *30*, *33*, *36*, *43*, *44*, *102*, 103–4
training plants, *42*, *44*
tree houses, 53, *53*
trellis, 93
tulips, 38, *124*
Tulipa 'Queen of Night', 18
Tulipa 'Spring Green', 18
tunnels, 53–4, *106*

V
valerians
red, 76
white (*Centranthus ruber* 'Albus'), *18*
Van Sweden, James, 25
vegetable plots, 50, 61, *61*, *63*, 87, *92*
vegetables, organic, 7, 61–3
Verbascum (mullein), *35*, *133*
Verbena bonariensis, 22, *112*, 131
Veronicastrum virginicum, 11
Versailles, 32
Viburnum tinus, 103
view, framing the, 100

W
walled gardens, 35

walls, 83, 87, 88, *92*, 93
concrete, *44*
stone-clad, 115
water features, *32*, 40, 84, 114–21
water gardens, 32
water lilies, *115*, *121*
wetland areas, 68, 71
White Gardens, 21
wildflower meadows, 7, 64, 68, *72*, *78*, 87
wildlife gardens, 64–79
willows, 35, 53, 54, 62, 93, *111*
Kilmarnock (*Salix caprea* 'Kilmarnock'), 103
witches' balls, *108*
wood, 88, 91, 93, 104, *106*
woodland gardens, 87

Y
yarrow *see* Achillea
yew (*Taxus baccata*), *30*, *39*, 44, 48, *87*, *90*, 94
Irish (*Taxus baccata* 'Fastigiata'), 48
York stone, 38

Z
Zantedeschia aethiopica (arum lily), *119*
Zen gardens, 40

acknowledgments

We would both like to thank the many garden owners and designers who so kindly allowed us to feature their homes and work in this book – it goes without saying that without them, this book would never have been possible. Many were also extremely generous with their time during our visits, and Melanie would particularly like to thank the people who allowed her to stay with them while she was photographing the gardens. So enormous thanks to: Peter and Sandra Aitken-Quack, Mart Barlow, Riet Brinkhof and Joop Van Den Berk, Tania Compton, Laura Cooper and Nick Taggart, Peter Farrell and family, Connie Haydon, James and Anne Hepworth and Anthony Brooks, Ivan Hicks, Jan Howard, Nancy Goslee Power, Isabelle Greene, Ineke Greve, Judy Kameon, Pam and Peter Lewis, Niall Manning and Alastair Morton, Christina and Nigel Oates, Sarah Raven and Adam Nicolson, Jim Reynolds, Marc Schoellen, Daphne Shackleton, Tom Stuart-Smith and family, Carol Valentine, Derry Watkins and Peter Clegg, David Wheeler and Simon Dorrell. Melanie would like to say an extra special thank you to Frances Anderton in Los Angeles for helping with gardening contacts and for having her to stay for ten days while she photographed. Elspeth would like to give a big thank you to Marianne Majerus for putting her in touch with Marc Schoellen in Luxembourg. And last but not least, we are extremely grateful to everyone at Ryland Peters and Small who has helped put the book together and especially Alison Starling who first approached us with the idea.

Elspeth Thompson and Melanie Eclare